**TEACHER'S PET PUBLICATIONS**

PUZZLE PACK
for
The Red Pony

based on the book by
John Steinbeck

Written by
William T. Collins

© 2005 Teacher's Pet Publications
All Rights Reserved

The materials in this packet are copyrighted
by Teacher's Pet Publications, Inc.

These pages may be duplicated by the purchaser
for use in the purchaser's own classroom.

Copying any of these materials and distributing them
for any other purpose is a violation of the copyright laws.

© 2005 Teacher's Pet Publications, Inc.
www.tpet.com

Red Pony Word List

No.	Word	Clue/Definition
1.	BILLY	____ Buck; ranch hand
2.	BUZZARD	Jody beat it to death
3.	CARL	Jody's father
4.	CENTER	The brush line where there was a patch of perpetually green grass was Jody's ____ point
5.	CHORES	Jobs Jody had to do on the ranch
6.	COLT	Baby horse
7.	DEMON	Black ____; the colt
8.	DIE	Gitano came home to do this
9.	EASTER	Carl's old horse
10.	FALLIBLE	Billy looked away....He had no right to be ____
11.	GABILAN	The red pony
12.	GIFT	Section I: The ____
13.	GITANO	Mexican man who came home to die
14.	HORSE	Easter, for example
15.	JODY	He got a pony
16.	LEADER	Section IV: The ____ of the People
17.	LEMON	Jody asked for only one
18.	MICE	Jody kills ____ in the haystack
19.	MISERY	Old things ought to be put out of their ___
20.	MOUNTAINS	Section II: The Great ____
21.	NELLIE	Mare who died berthing
22.	PONY	The Red ____
23.	PRIDE	Mrs. Tiflin felt 'a curious ____ rise up in her'
24.	PROMISE	Section III: The ____
25.	RANCH	Place where Billy Buck works
26.	RED	Color of the pony
27.	REPULSIVE	The black cypress tree where pigs were slaughtered was ____ to Jody
28.	ROCKS	Jody threw them at birds
29.	SALINAS	Mr. Tiflin sold cows & bought a pony there
30.	STALLION	Male horse
31.	STEINBECK	Author
32.	TRAINING	The red pony resented ____
33.	TRAP	Jody snapped a dog's nose in one
34.	WESTERING	It has died out of the people

Red Pony Fill In The Blanks 1

_____

_____

_____

_____

_____

_____

_____

_____

_____

_____

_____

_____

_____

_____

_____

_____

_____

_____

_____

_____

1. The Red ____
2. Mrs. Tiflin felt 'a curious ____ rise up in her'
3. ____ Buck; ranch hand
4. Place where Billy Buck works
5. Section II: The Great ____
6. Jody's father
7. Jobs Jody had to do on the ranch
8. Section I: The ____
9. Gitano came home to do this
10. Jody asked for only one
11. It has died out of the people
12. Color of the pony
13. Billy looked away....He had no right to be ____
14. He got a pony
15. The black cypress tree where pigs were slaughtered was ____ to Jody
16. The red pony resented ____
17. Mr. Tiflin sold cows & bought a pony there
18. Jody snapped a dog's nose in one
19. The red pony
20. Black ____; the colt

Red Pony Fill In The Blanks 1 Answer Key

PONY	1. The Red ____
PRIDE	2. Mrs. Tiflin felt 'a curious ____ rise up in her'
BILLY	3. ____ Buck; ranch hand
RANCH	4. Place where Billy Buck works
MOUNTAINS	5. Section II: The Great ____
CARL	6. Jody's father
CHORES	7. Jobs Jody had to do on the ranch
GIFT	8. Section I: The ____
DIE	9. Gitano came home to do this
LEMON	10. Jody asked for only one
WESTERING	11. It has died out of the people
RED	12. Color of the pony
FALLIBLE	13. Billy looked away....He had no right to be ____
JODY	14. He got a pony
REPULSIVE	15. The black cypress tree where pigs were slaughtered was ____ to Jody
TRAINING	16. The red pony resented ____
SALINAS	17. Mr. Tiflin sold cows & bought a pony there
TRAP	18. Jody snapped a dog's nose in one
GABILAN	19. The red pony
DEMON	20. Black ____; the colt

Copyrighted

Red Pony Fill In The Blanks 2

_____ 1. Place where Billy Buck works

_____ 2. Section IV: The ____ of the People

_____ 3. Section I: The ____

_____ 4. Male horse

_____ 5. It has died out of the people

_____ 6. Billy looked away....He had no right to be ____

_____ 7. Jody threw them at birds

_____ 8. Jobs Jody had to do on the ranch

_____ 9. The Red ____

_____ 10. Black ____; the colt

_____ 11. Color of the pony

_____ 12. Baby horse

_____ 13. The red pony resented ____

_____ 14. He got a pony

_____ 15. The red pony

_____ 16. Old things ought to be put out of their ____

_____ 17. ____ Buck; ranch hand

_____ 18. Gitano came home to do this

_____ 19. Jody snapped a dog's nose in one

_____ 20. Mare who died berthing

Red Pony Fill In The Blanks 2 Answer Key

RANCH	1. Place where Billy Buck works
LEADER	2. Section IV: The ____ of the People
GIFT	3. Section I: The ____
STALLION	4. Male horse
WESTERING	5. It has died out of the people
FALLIBLE	6. Billy looked away....He had no right to be ____
ROCKS	7. Jody threw them at birds
CHORES	8. Jobs Jody had to do on the ranch
PONY	9. The Red ____
DEMON	10. Black ____; the colt
RED	11. Color of the pony
COLT	12. Baby horse
TRAINING	13. The red pony resented ____
JODY	14. He got a pony
GABILAN	15. The red pony
MISERY	16. Old things ought to be put out of their ___
BILLY	17. ____ Buck; ranch hand
DIE	18. Gitano came home to do this
TRAP	19. Jody snapped a dog's nose in one
NELLIE	20. Mare who died berthing

Red Pony Fill In The Blanks 3

_____   1. The red pony
_____   2. Section I: The ____
_____   3. ____ Buck; ranch hand
_____   4. Jody threw them at birds
_____   5. The red pony resented ____
_____   6. Jody asked for only one
_____   7. Jody snapped a dog's nose in one
_____   8. Mr. Tiflin sold cows & bought a pony there
_____   9. Black ____; the colt
_____   10. Jobs Jody had to do on the ranch
_____   11. It has died out of the people
_____   12. Billy looked away....He had no right to be ____
_____   13. The black cypress tree where pigs were slaughtered was ____ to Jody
                        14. Carl's old horse
_____   15. Place where Billy Buck works
_____   16. Jody beat it to death
_____   17. Old things ought to be put out of their ___
_____   18. Section IV: The ____ of the People
_____   19. Author
_____   20. He got a pony

Red Pony Fill In The Blanks 3 Answer Key

GABILAN	1. The red pony
GIFT	2. Section I: The ____
BILLY	3. ____ Buck; ranch hand
ROCKS	4. Jody threw them at birds
TRAINING	5. The red pony resented ____
LEMON	6. Jody asked for only one
TRAP	7. Jody snapped a dog's nose in one
SALINAS	8. Mr. Tiflin sold cows & bought a pony there
DEMON	9. Black ____; the colt
CHORES	10. Jobs Jody had to do on the ranch
WESTERING	11. It has died out of the people
FALLIBLE	12. Billy looked away....He had no right to be ____
REPULSIVE	13. The black cypress tree where pigs were slaughtered was ____ to Jody
EASTER	14. Carl's old horse
RANCH	15. Place where Billy Buck works
BUZZARD	16. Jody beat it to death
MISERY	17. Old things ought to be put out of their ____
LEADER	18. Section IV: The ____ of the People
STEINBECK	19. Author
JODY	20. He got a pony

Red Pony Fill In The Blanks 4

_____ 1. Male horse
_____ 2. Jody asked for only one
_____ 3. Jody threw them at birds
_____ 4. Section II: The Great ____
_____ 5. The red pony resented ____
_____ 6. Old things ought to be put out of their ___
_____ 7. The red pony
_____ 8. The black cypress tree where pigs were slaughtered was ____ to Jody
_____ 9. Jody beat it to death
_____ 10. Easter, for example
_____ 11. Mare who died berthing
_____ 12. Mr. Tiflin sold cows & bought a pony there
_____ 13. The Red ____
_____ 14. Gitano came home to do this
_____ 15. Black ____; the colt
_____ 16. ____ Buck; ranch hand
_____ 17. Section IV: The ____ of the People
_____ 18. Jody snapped a dog's nose in one
_____ 19. He got a pony
_____ 20. Jody kills ____ in the haystack

Red Pony Fill In The Blanks 4 Answer Key

STALLION	1. Male horse
LEMON	2. Jody asked for only one
ROCKS	3. Jody threw them at birds
MOUNTAINS	4. Section II: The Great ____
TRAINING	5. The red pony resented ____
MISERY	6. Old things ought to be put out of their ___
GABILAN	7. The red pony
REPULSIVE	8. The black cypress tree where pigs were slaughtered was ____ to Jody
BUZZARD	9. Jody beat it to death
HORSE	10. Easter, for example
NELLIE	11. Mare who died berthing
SALINAS	12. Mr. Tiflin sold cows & bought a pony there
PONY	13. The Red ____
DIE	14. Gitano came home to do this
DEMON	15. Black ____; the colt
BILLY	16. ____ Buck; ranch hand
LEADER	17. Section IV: The ____ of the People
TRAP	18. Jody snapped a dog's nose in one
JODY	19. He got a pony
MICE	20. Jody kills ____ in the haystack

Red Pony Matching 1

___ 1. TRAP   A. Author
___ 2. GABILAN   B. Jody asked for only one
___ 3. LEADER   C. Jobs Jody had to do on the ranch
___ 4. TRAINING   D. Jody's father
___ 5. CENTER   E. The brush line where there was a patch of perpetually green grass was Jody's ____ point
___ 6. EASTER   F. The red pony resented ____
___ 7. DEMON   G. ____ Buck; ranch hand
___ 8. SALINAS   H. Section IV: The ____ of the People
___ 9. CHORES   I. The Red ____
___ 10. BUZZARD   J. Jody kills ____ in the haystack
___ 11. HORSE   K. Old things ought to be put out of their ____
___ 12. MISERY   L. He got a pony
___ 13. CARL   M. Color of the pony
___ 14. PROMISE   N. Billy looked away....He had no right to be ____
___ 15. REPULSIVE   O. Mexican man who came home to die
___ 16. PONY   P. Easter, for example
___ 17. STALLION   Q. The red pony
___ 18. JODY   R. Carl's old horse
___ 19. BILLY   S. Jody snapped a dog's nose in one
___ 20. STEINBECK   T. Mr. Tiflin sold cows & bought a pony there
___ 21. GITANO   U. Male horse
___ 22. RED   V. Black ____; the colt
___ 23. LEMON   W. The black cypress tree where pigs were slaughtered was ____ to Jody
___ 24. FALLIBLE   X. Section III: The ____
___ 25. MICE   Y. Jody beat it to death

Red Pony Matching 1 Answer Key

S - 1. TRAP	A.	Author
Q - 2. GABILAN	B.	Jody asked for only one
H - 3. LEADER	C.	Jobs Jody had to do on the ranch
F - 4. TRAINING	D.	Jody's father
E - 5. CENTER	E.	The brush line where there was a patch of perpetually green grass was Jody's ____ point
R - 6. EASTER	F.	The red pony resented ____
V - 7. DEMON	G.	____ Buck; ranch hand
T - 8. SALINAS	H.	Section IV: The ____ of the People
C - 9. CHORES	I.	The Red ____
Y -10. BUZZARD	J.	Jody kills ____ in the haystack
P -11. HORSE	K.	Old things ought to be put out of their ___
K -12. MISERY	L.	He got a pony
D -13. CARL	M.	Color of the pony
X -14. PROMISE	N.	Billy looked away....He had no right to be ____
W -15. REPULSIVE	O.	Mexican man who came home to die
I - 16. PONY	P.	Easter, for example
U -17. STALLION	Q.	The red pony
L - 18. JODY	R.	Carl's old horse
G -19. BILLY	S.	Jody snapped a dog's nose in one
A -20. STEINBECK	T.	Mr. Tiflin sold cows & bought a pony there
O -21. GITANO	U.	Male horse
M -22. RED	V.	Black ____; the colt
B -23. LEMON	W.	The black cypress tree where pigs were slaughtered was ____ to Jody
N -24. FALLIBLE	X.	Section III: The ____
J - 25. MICE	Y.	Jody beat it to death

Copyrighted

Red Pony Matching 2

___ 1. STALLION   A. The red pony

___ 2. LEADER   B. It has died out of the people

___ 3. EASTER   C. The brush line where there was a patch of perpetually green grass was Jody's ____ point

___ 4. LEMON   D. Jody kills ____ in the haystack

___ 5. GITANO   E. Mr. Tiflin sold cows & bought a pony there

___ 6. JODY   F. Carl's old horse

___ 7. NELLIE   G. Mexican man who came home to die

___ 8. CARL   H. Jody threw them at birds

___ 9. PONY   I. Section III: The ____

___ 10. STEINBECK   J. Author

___ 11. ROCKS   K. Mrs. Tiflin felt 'a curious ____ rise up in her'

___ 12. WESTERING   L. Easter, for example

___ 13. MISERY   M. Jody's father

___ 14. RANCH   N. Section IV: The ____ of the People

___ 15. TRAP   O. Color of the pony

___ 16. CENTER   P. Old things ought to be put out of their ___

___ 17. PROMISE   Q. Jody beat it to death

___ 18. BUZZARD   R. The Red ____

___ 19. RED   S. Black ____; the colt

___ 20. DEMON   T. Jody snapped a dog's nose in one

___ 21. SALINAS   U. He got a pony

___ 22. MICE   V. Place where Billy Buck works

___ 23. GABILAN   W. Male horse

___ 24. HORSE   X. Jody asked for only one

___ 25. PRIDE   Y. Mare who died berthing

Red Pony Matching 2 Answer Key

W - 1. STALLION	A.	The red pony
N - 2. LEADER	B.	It has died out of the people
F - 3. EASTER	C.	The brush line where there was a patch of perpetually green grass was Jody's ____ point
X - 4. LEMON	D.	Jody kills ____ in the haystack
G - 5. GITANO	E.	Mr. Tiflin sold cows & bought a pony there
U - 6. JODY	F.	Carl's old horse
Y - 7. NELLIE	G.	Mexican man who came home to die
M - 8. CARL	H.	Jody threw them at birds
R - 9. PONY	I.	Section III: The ____
J - 10. STEINBECK	J.	Author
H - 11. ROCKS	K.	Mrs. Tiflin felt 'a curious ____ rise up in her'
B - 12. WESTERING	L.	Easter, for example
P - 13. MISERY	M.	Jody's father
V - 14. RANCH	N.	Section IV: The ____ of the People
T - 15. TRAP	O.	Color of the pony
C - 16. CENTER	P.	Old things ought to be put out of their ____
I - 17. PROMISE	Q.	Jody beat it to death
Q - 18. BUZZARD	R.	The Red ____
O - 19. RED	S.	Black ____; the colt
S - 20. DEMON	T.	Jody snapped a dog's nose in one
E - 21. SALINAS	U.	He got a pony
D - 22. MICE	V.	Place where Billy Buck works
A - 23. GABILAN	W.	Male horse
L - 24. HORSE	X.	Jody asked for only one
K - 25. PRIDE	Y.	Mare who died berthing

Red Pony Matching 3

___ 1. DEMON A. Jody's father
___ 2. SALINAS B. Mr. Tiflin sold cows & bought a pony there
___ 3. MOUNTAINS C. ____ Buck; ranch hand
___ 4. STEINBECK D. Jody snapped a dog's nose in one
___ 5. EASTER E. The red pony resented ____
___ 6. STALLION F. Section II: The Great ____
___ 7. TRAINING G. Mare who died berthing
___ 8. TRAP H. Jody beat it to death
___ 9. GITANO I. The brush line where there was a patch of perpetually green grass was Jody's ____ point
___ 10. LEADER J. Section III: The ____
___ 11. GABILAN K. Author
___ 12. BILLY L. Baby horse
___ 13. RED M. It has died out of the people
___ 14. CENTER N. Carl's old horse
___ 15. PROMISE O. Billy looked away....He had no right to be ____
___ 16. MISERY P. Old things ought to be put out of their ___
___ 17. COLT Q. Male horse
___ 18. BUZZARD R. Section IV: The ____ of the People
___ 19. DIE S. Jody asked for only one
___ 20. LEMON T. Mexican man who came home to die
___ 21. FALLIBLE U. Easter, for example
___ 22. CARL V. Color of the pony
___ 23. HORSE W. The red pony
___ 24. WESTERING X. Black ____; the colt
___ 25. NELLIE Y. Gitano came home to do this

Red Pony Matching 3 Answer Key

X - 1. DEMON	A.	Jody's father
B - 2. SALINAS	B.	Mr. Tiflin sold cows & bought a pony there
F - 3. MOUNTAINS	C.	____ Buck; ranch hand
K - 4. STEINBECK	D.	Jody snapped a dog's nose in one
N - 5. EASTER	E.	The red pony resented ____
Q - 6. STALLION	F.	Section II: The Great ____
E - 7. TRAINING	G.	Mare who died berthing
D - 8. TRAP	H.	Jody beat it to death
T - 9. GITANO	I.	The brush line where there was a patch of perpetually green grass was Jody's ____ point
R - 10. LEADER	J.	Section III: The ____
W - 11. GABILAN	K.	Author
C - 12. BILLY	L.	Baby horse
V - 13. RED	M.	It has died out of the people
I - 14. CENTER	N.	Carl's old horse
J - 15. PROMISE	O.	Billy looked away....He had no right to be ____
P - 16. MISERY	P.	Old things ought to be put out of their ___
L - 17. COLT	Q.	Male horse
H - 18. BUZZARD	R.	Section IV: The ____ of the People
Y - 19. DIE	S.	Jody asked for only one
S - 20. LEMON	T.	Mexican man who came home to die
O - 21. FALLIBLE	U.	Easter, for example
A - 22. CARL	V.	Color of the pony
U - 23. HORSE	W.	The red pony
M - 24. WESTERING	X.	Black ____; the colt
G - 25. NELLIE	Y.	Gitano came home to do this

Red Pony Matching 4

___ 1. DIE   A. The Red ____
___ 2. CHORES   B. Mare who died berthing
___ 3. MISERY   C. Section II: The Great ____
___ 4. JODY   D. Male horse
___ 5. ROCKS   E. Carl's old horse
___ 6. GITANO   F. Jobs Jody had to do on the ranch
___ 7. RANCH   G. Place where Billy Buck works
___ 8. NELLIE   H. Old things ought to be put out of their ___
___ 9. STALLION   I. Mrs. Tiflin felt 'a curious ____ rise up in her'
___10. FALLIBLE   J. He got a pony
___11. TRAINING   K. Baby horse
___12. MOUNTAINS   L. The red pony resented ____
___13. RED   M. Mexican man who came home to die
___14. GIFT   N. Jody threw them at birds
___15. COLT   O. Color of the pony
___16. HORSE   P. Section IV: The ____ of the People
___17. SALINAS   Q. Jody beat it to death
___18. WESTERING   R. Mr. Tiflin sold cows & bought a pony there
___19. CENTER   S. Gitano came home to do this
___20. EASTER   T. Easter, for example
___21. PONY   U. Black ____; the colt
___22. PRIDE   V. Billy looked away....He had no right to be ____
___23. LEADER   W. It has died out of the people
___24. BUZZARD   X. The brush line where there was a patch of perpetually green grass was Jody's ____ point
___25. DEMON   Y. Section I: The ____

Red Pony Matching 4 Answer Key

S - 1. DIE	A.	The Red ____
F - 2. CHORES	B.	Mare who died berthing
H - 3. MISERY	C.	Section II: The Great ____
J - 4. JODY	D.	Male horse
N - 5. ROCKS	E.	Carl's old horse
M - 6. GITANO	F.	Jobs Jody had to do on the ranch
G - 7. RANCH	G.	Place where Billy Buck works
B - 8. NELLIE	H.	Old things ought to be put out of their ____
D - 9. STALLION	I.	Mrs. Tiflin felt 'a curious ____ rise up in her'
V -10. FALLIBLE	J.	He got a pony
L -11. TRAINING	K.	Baby horse
C -12. MOUNTAINS	L.	The red pony resented ____
O -13. RED	M.	Mexican man who came home to die
Y -14. GIFT	N.	Jody threw them at birds
K -15. COLT	O.	Color of the pony
T -16. HORSE	P.	Section IV: The ____ of the People
R -17. SALINAS	Q.	Jody beat it to death
W -18. WESTERING	R.	Mr. Tiflin sold cows & bought a pony there
X -19. CENTER	S.	Gitano came home to do this
E -20. EASTER	T.	Easter, for example
A -21. PONY	U.	Black ____; the colt
I -22. PRIDE	V.	Billy looked away....He had no right to be ____
P -23. LEADER	W.	It has died out of the people
Q -24. BUZZARD	X.	The brush line where there was a patch of perpetually green grass was Jody's ____ point
U -25. DEMON	Y.	Section I: The ____

Red Pony Magic Squares 1

Match the definition with the vocabulary word. Put your answers in the magic squares below. When your answers are correct, all columns and rows will add to the same number.

A. DEMON
B. MISERY
C. MICE
D. JODY
E. LEADER
F. GITANO
G. ROCKS
H. EASTER
I. RED
J. BILLY
K. WESTERING
L. REPULSIVE
M. PRIDE
N. CARL
O. PONY
P. STEINBECK

1. Jody kills ____ in the haystack
2. ____ Buck; ranch hand
3. Mexican man who came home to die
4. The Red ____
5. Author
6. Section IV: The ____ of the People
7. Color of the pony
8. He got a pony
9. Mrs. Tiflin felt 'a curious ____ rise up in her'
10. Carl's old horse
11. The black cypress tree where pigs were slaughtered was ____ to Jody
12. Black ____; the colt
13. Old things ought to be put out of their ____
14. It has died out of the people
15. Jody threw them at birds
16. Jody's father

A=	B=	C=	D=
E=	F=	G=	H=
I=	J=	K=	L=
M=	N=	O=	P=

Red Pony Magic Squares 1 Answer Key

Match the definition with the vocabulary word. Put your answers in the magic squares below. When your answers are correct, all columns and rows will add to the same number.

A. DEMON
B. MISERY
C. MICE
D. JODY

E. LEADER
F. GITANO
G. ROCKS
H. EASTER

I. RED
J. BILLY
K. WESTERING
L. REPULSIVE

M. PRIDE
N. CARL
O. PONY
P. STEINBECK

1. Jody kills ____ in the haystack
2. ____ Buck; ranch hand
3. Mexican man who came home to die
4. The Red ____
5. Author
6. Section IV: The ____ of the People
7. Color of the pony
8. He got a pony
9. Mrs. Tiflin felt 'a curious ____ rise up in her'
10. Carl's old horse
11. The black cypress tree where pigs were slaughtered was ____ to Jody
12. Black ____; the colt
13. Old things ought to be put out of their ____
14. It has died out of the people
15. Jody threw them at birds
16. Jody's father

A=12	B=13	C=1	D=8
E=6	F=3	G=15	H=10
I=7	J=2	K=14	L=11
M=9	N=16	O=4	P=5

Red Pony Magic Squares 2

Match the definition with the vocabulary word. Put your answers in the magic squares below. When your answers are correct, all columns and rows will add to the same number.

A. COLT   E. JODY   I. FALLIBLE   M. CENTER
B. PRIDE   F. BILLY   J. DIE   N. GIFT
C. PONY   G. STEINBECK   K. RED   O. DEMON
D. MICE   H. HORSE   L. SALINAS   P. GITANO

1. Easter, for example
2. The brush line where there was a patch of perpetually green grass was Jody's ____ point
3. Mrs. Tiflin felt 'a curious ____ rise up in her'
4. Color of the pony
5. Gitano came home to do this
6. The Red ____
7. Mexican man who came home to die
8. He got a pony
9. Black ____; the colt
10. ____ Buck; ranch hand
11. Billy looked away....He had no right to be ____
12. Jody kills ____ in the haystack
13. Baby horse
14. Mr. Tiflin sold cows & bought a pony there
15. Author
16. Section I: The ____

A=	B=	C=	D=
E=	F=	G=	H=
I=	J=	K=	L=
M=	N=	O=	P=

Red Pony Magic Squares 2 Answer Key

Match the definition with the vocabulary word. Put your answers in the magic squares below. When your answers are correct, all columns and rows will add to the same number.

A. COLT
B. PRIDE
C. PONY
D. MICE
E. JODY
F. BILLY
G. STEINBECK
H. HORSE
I. FALLIBLE
J. DIE
K. RED
L. SALINAS
M. CENTER
N. GIFT
O. DEMON
P. GITANO

1. Easter, for example
2. The brush line where there was a patch of perpetually green grass was Jody's ____ point
3. Mrs. Tiflin felt 'a curious ____ rise up in her'
4. Color of the pony
5. Gitano came home to do this
6. The Red ____
7. Mexican man who came home to die
8. He got a pony
9. Black ____; the colt
10. ____ Buck; ranch hand
11. Billy looked away....He had no right to be ____
12. Jody kills ____ in the haystack
13. Baby horse
14. Mr. Tiflin sold cows & bought a pony there
15. Author
16. Section I: The ____

A=13	B=3	C=6	D=12
E=8	F=10	G=15	H=1
I=11	J=5	K=4	L=14
M=2	N=16	O=9	P=7

Red Pony Magic Squares 3

Match the definition with the vocabulary word. Put your answers in the magic squares below. When your answers are correct, all columns and rows will add to the same number.

A. WESTERING E. RANCH   I. MOUNTAINS M. PROMISE
B. STEINBECK F. EASTER   J. DEMON   N. HORSE
C. NELLIE   G. JODY   K. TRAP   O. CHORES
D. PRIDE   H. CARL   L. GABILAN   P. DIE

1. It has died out of the people
2. Easter, for example
3. Black ____; the colt
4. Place where Billy Buck works
5. He got a pony
6. The red pony
7. Gitano came home to do this
8. Mare who died berthing
9. Jobs Jody had to do on the ranch
10. Mrs. Tiflin felt 'a curious ____ rise up in her'
11. Jody's father
12. Jody snapped a dog's nose in one
13. Section II: The Great ____
14. Carl's old horse
15. Author
16. Section III: The ____

A=	B=	C=	D=
E=	F=	G=	H=
I=	J=	K=	L=
M=	N=	O=	P=

Red Pony Magic Squares 3 Answer Key

Match the definition with the vocabulary word. Put your answers in the magic squares below. When your answers are correct, all columns and rows will add to the same number.

A. WESTERING   E. RANCH   I. MOUNTAINS   M. PROMISE
B. STEINBECK   F. EASTER   J. DEMON   N. HORSE
C. NELLIE   G. JODY   K. TRAP   O. CHORES
D. PRIDE   H. CARL   L. GABILAN   P. DIE

1. It has died out of the people
2. Easter, for example
3. Black ____; the colt
4. Place where Billy Buck works
5. He got a pony
6. The red pony
7. Gitano came home to do this
8. Mare who died berthing
9. Jobs Jody had to do on the ranch
10. Mrs. Tiflin felt 'a curious ____ rise up in her'
11. Jody's father
12. Jody snapped a dog's nose in one
13. Section II: The Great ____
14. Carl's old horse
15. Author
16. Section III: The ____

A=1	B=15	C=8	D=10
E=4	F=14	G=5	H=11
I=13	J=3	K=12	L=6
M=16	N=2	O=9	P=7

Red Pony Magic Squares 4

Match the definition with the vocabulary word. Put your answers in the magic squares below. When your answers are correct, all columns and rows will add to the same number.

A. MISERY
B. STEINBECK
C. GABILAN
D. BUZZARD

E. RED
F. NELLIE
G. CHORES
H. PROMISE

I. COLT
J. CENTER
K. LEADER
L. LEMON

M. CARL
N. MOUNTAINS
O. STALLION
P. WESTERING

1. Jody's father
2. Mare who died berthing
3. Section III: The ____
4. Male horse
5. Jody asked for only one
6. The red pony
7. Old things ought to be put out of their ____
8. The brush line where there was a patch of perpetually green grass was Jody's ____ point
9. Section IV: The ____ of the People
10. Jody beat it to death
11. Author
12. Baby horse
13. Section II: The Great ____
14. Color of the pony
15. Jobs Jody had to do on the ranch
16. It has died out of the people

A=	B=	C=	D=
E=	F=	G=	H=
I=	J=	K=	L=
M=	N=	O=	P=

Red Pony Magic Squares 4 Answer Key

Match the definition with the vocabulary word. Put your answers in the magic squares below. When your answers are correct, all columns and rows will add to the same number.

A. MISERY   E. RED   I. COLT   M. CARL
B. STEINBECK   F. NELLIE   J. CENTER   N. MOUNTAINS
C. GABILAN   G. CHORES   K. LEADER   O. STALLION
D. BUZZARD   H. PROMISE   L. LEMON   P. WESTERING

1. Jody's father
2. Mare who died berthing
3. Section III: The _____
4. Male horse
5. Jody asked for only one
6. The red pony
7. Old things ought to be put out of their _____
8. The brush line where there was a patch of perpetually green grass was Jody's _____ point

9. Section IV: The _____ of the People
10. Jody beat it to death
11. Author
12. Baby horse
13. Section II: The Great _____
14. Color of the pony
15. Jobs Jody had to do on the ranch
16. It has died out of the people

A=7	B=11	C=6	D=10
E=14	F=2	G=15	H=3
I=12	J=8	K=9	L=5
M=1	N=13	O=4	P=16

Red Pony Word Search 1

Words are placed backwards, forward, diagonally, up and down. Clues listed below can help you find the words. Circle the hidden vocabulary words in the maze.

```
S T A L L I O N G R E B Q C M R A N C H
A F B E G M L C S M A L U T F I T Y M R
L A T A L R S B D B S R M Z Z F C M O N
I L P D D V Q H X X T P G Q Z K N E U W
N L R E P U L S I V E Z R Y V A F Z N G
A I R R N Y G H T G R H D I L C R P T P
S B S P L W Y C J F W S N I D M D D A G
N L H T L Q M Y L X V F B X C E X J I F
W E F C H O R E S W N A F V T N M D N G
N I F R B K Z J T D G Z K P L K J V S X
G P P W K W D D V N S D D M F G L S F W
B S Y Y N E W S J D R V M F B G F L N P
Z W F B Y S C H V D R G C P H T S W P P
H X W D L T M R Q Z Z D R W F R N L G Z
W L T J Y E F D V C S X P M X Z G Y F J
V D T T T R J R W E D C R W G N N B L N
P Q G R N I O N J N M L O M I V W B E C
T S G A E N D Q R T Q B M N I L E V M C
X C C P L G Y K C E B N I E T S K C O R
Z P O P L E X V R R D A S L R Y E A N P
L N L Z I T T F Y G R Z E O L Y Q R B K
Y S T D E M O N A T I G H X B Y H L Y J
```

Author (9)
Baby horse (4)
Billy looked away....He had no right to be ____ (8)
Black ____; the colt (5)
Carl's old horse (6)
Color of the pony (3)
Easter, for example (5)
Gitano came home to do this (3)
He got a pony (4)
It has died out of the people (9)
Jobs Jody had to do on the ranch (6)
Jody asked for only one (5)
Jody beat it to death (7)
Jody kills ____ in the haystack (4)
Jody snapped a dog's nose in one (4)
Jody threw them at birds (5)
Jody's father (4)
Male horse (8)
Mare who died berthing (6)
Mexican man who came home to die (6)

Mr. Tiflin sold cows & bought a pony there (7)
Mrs. Tiflin felt 'a curious ____ rise up in her' (5)
Old things ought to be put out of their ___ (6)
Place where Billy Buck works (5)
Section I: The ____ (4)
Section II: The Great ____ (9)
Section III: The ____ (7)
Section IV: The ____ of the People (6)
The Red ____ (4)
The black cypress tree where pigs were slaughtered was ____ to Jody (9)
The brush line where there was a patch of perpetually green grass was Jody's ____ point (6)
The red pony (7)
The red pony resented ____ (8)
____ Buck; ranch hand (5)

Red Pony Word Search 1 Answer Key

Words are placed backwards, forward, diagonally, up and down. Clues listed below can help you find the words. Circle the hidden vocabulary words in the maze.

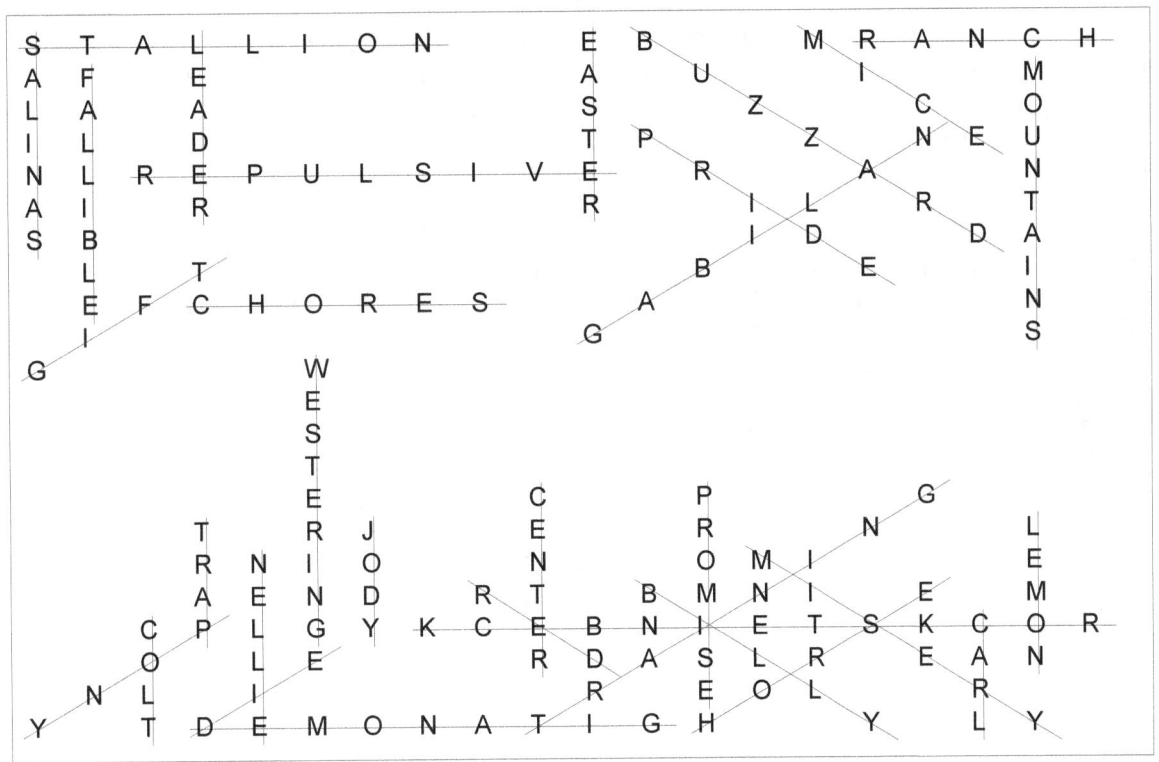

Author (9)
Baby horse (4)
Billy looked away....He had no right to be ____ (8)
Black ____; the colt (5)
Carl's old horse (6)
Color of the pony (3)
Easter, for example (5)
Gitano came home to do this (3)
He got a pony (4)
It has died out of the people (9)
Jobs Jody had to do on the ranch (6)
Jody asked for only one (5)
Jody beat it to death (7)
Jody kills ____ in the haystack (4)
Jody snapped a dog's nose in one (4)
Jody threw them at birds (5)
Jody's father (4)
Male horse (8)
Mare who died berthing (6)
Mexican man who came home to die (6)

Mr. Tiflin sold cows & bought a pony there (7)
Mrs. Tiflin felt 'a curious ____ rise up in her' (5)
Old things ought to be put out of their ____ (6)
Place where Billy Buck works (5)
Section I: The ____ (4)
Section II: The Great ____ (9)
Section III: The ____ (7)
Section IV: The ____ of the People (6)
The Red ____ (4)
The black cypress tree where pigs were slaughtered was ____ to Jody (9)
The brush line where there was a patch of perpetually green grass was Jody's ____ point (6)
The red pony (7)
The red pony resented ____ (8)
____ Buck; ranch hand (5)

Red Pony Word Search 2

Words are placed backwards, forward, diagonally, up and down. Clues listed below can help you find the words. Circle the hidden vocabulary words in the maze.

```
B I L L Y D E M O N Y N M G I F T J Q C
U C Q E X C Q G R R A H B R F A K P R Y
Z C G A J B N D E L Z W S R Q L Q S L S
Z P P D X J S S I G X B G C L L V R Y M
A S Z E L F I B P R E P U L S I V E R Q
R D T R C M A G Q C H Q R C T B Y B P B
D Q A E F G M B I L G D D X N L Z J M J
M C X V I M B M T C X C V K R E S J H P
H T W D Q N D T V W R Q K Q O W J N P X
M N R T X F B B M H V G D Z C M D M P M
F T M D R N T E P X S Q M Q K C S W J Y
Q B R F G A F V C Z O B W D S R T T C L
Y Z K S V R I S T K N L B X N G A T B H
W F P X W V Z N W D A B L P F P L X X Y
J Y B D E G V H I J T T S O C Y L H K X
M K P Q S P P G G N I P Q N G H I C Q W
R B R G T R R C L L G H D Y K Y O Z S M
N H J X E C O E P X O G V K P L N R Q H
F C C T R D M N G R Y K G H T R J T E H
L N S T I O I T S V G P V Y D V I O T S
S A L I N A S E M O U N T A I N S D D W
E R E D G W E R N E L L I E T R A P E Y
```

Author (9)
Baby horse (4)
Billy looked away....He had no right to be ____ (8)
Black ____; the colt (5)
Carl's old horse (6)
Color of the pony (3)
Easter, for example (5)
Gitano came home to do this (3)
He got a pony (4)
It has died out of the people (9)
Jobs Jody had to do on the ranch (6)
Jody asked for only one (5)
Jody beat it to death (7)
Jody kills ____ in the haystack (4)
Jody snapped a dog's nose in one (4)
Jody threw them at birds (5)
Jody's father (4)
Male horse (8)
Mare who died berthing (6)
Mexican man who came home to die (6)

Mr. Tiflin sold cows & bought a pony there (7)
Mrs. Tiflin felt 'a curious ____ rise up in her' (5)
Old things ought to be put out of their ___ (6)
Place where Billy Buck works (5)
Section I: The ____ (4)
Section II: The Great ____ (9)
Section III: The ____ (7)
Section IV: The ____ of the People (6)
The Red ____ (4)
The black cypress tree where pigs were slaughtered was ____ to Jody (9)
The brush line where there was a patch of perpetually green grass was Jody's ____ point (6)
The red pony (7)
The red pony resented ____ (8)
____ Buck; ranch hand (5)

Red Pony Word Search 2 Answer Key

Words are placed backwards, forward, diagonally, up and down. Clues listed below can help you find the words. Circle the hidden vocabulary words in the maze.

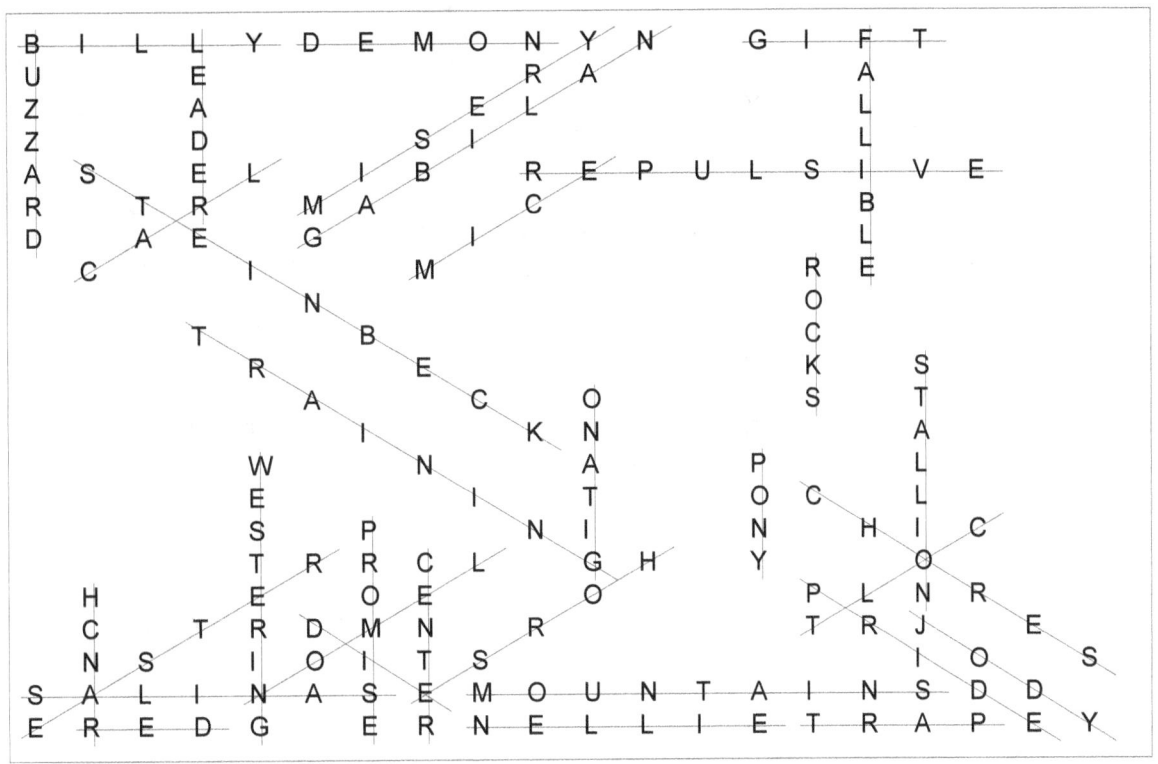

Author (9)
Baby horse (4)
Billy looked away....He had no right to be ____ (8)
Black ____; the colt (5)
Carl's old horse (6)
Color of the pony (3)
Easter, for example (5)
Gitano came home to do this (3)
He got a pony (4)
It has died out of the people (9)
Jobs Jody had to do on the ranch (6)
Jody asked for only one (5)
Jody beat it to death (7)
Jody kills ____ in the haystack (4)
Jody snapped a dog's nose in one (4)
Jody threw them at birds (5)
Jody's father (4)
Male horse (8)
Mare who died berthing (6)
Mexican man who came home to die (6)

Mr. Tiflin sold cows & bought a pony there (7)
Mrs. Tiflin felt 'a curious ____ rise up in her' (5)
Old things ought to be put out of their ____ (6)
Place where Billy Buck works (5)
Section I: The ____ (4)
Section II: The Great ____ (9)
Section III: The ____ (7)
Section IV: The ____ of the People (6)
The Red ____ (4)
The black cypress tree where pigs were slaughtered was ____ to Jody (9)
The brush line where there was a patch of perpetually green grass was Jody's ____ point (6)
The red pony (7)
The red pony resented ____ (8)
____ Buck; ranch hand (5)

Red Pony Word Search 3

Words are placed backwards, forward, diagonally, up and down. Words listed below are included in the maze. Circle the hidden vocabulary words in the maze.

```
G G S T W S S T R A P J N P S S L J L S
V I L X H W T V W S G Q F Z T S M X P N
N O T C X R A Y D Y C P C L E G J P B M
C G G A B I L A N Z G T Q G I K J D T M
P Y V D N G L M R Q D P N N Y T T B V
W K X V B O I B N K L I S V B M J Q G L
R S J M J W O L S W N B R X E R T X V P
Y G K Y Z K N R N I N D D Z C N S F K Q
X G D V R Z W G A Q N M L Q K X L V K Z
M R J X Y E K R W D D C B S S W W F J C
C G C Z F S T M Q B F H J J A Z E N R P
V M E W C I D Q I Z T C B F L E S T E C
W W N M N M P C C S P H I C I L T Z T Z
C J T R V O P A B D E O L L N K E G S T
G V E V L R H R E H I R L M A G R N A D
R T R R E P U L S I V E Y E S M I C E D
A L P S Y M B P E S N S G K M A N R D Y
N R R T H I M X S A X Z C K T O G R I S
C O Q Y L T K Y S P D O R N P S N X R W
H L D L G I F T F S R E U P O N Y B P N
Z O A D C Q K R X Y Y O R X H W J N R Y
J F M D E M O N L R M B U Z Z A R D M L
```

BILLY	DIE	JODY	PONY	SALINAS
BUZZARD	EASTER	LEADER	PRIDE	STALLION
CARL	FALLIBLE	LEMON	PROMISE	STEINBECK
CENTER	GABILAN	MICE	RANCH	TRAINING
CHORES	GIFT	MISERY	RED	TRAP
COLT	GITANO	MOUNTAINS	REPULSIVE	WESTERING
DEMON	HORSE	NELLIE	ROCKS	

Red Pony Word Search 3 Answer Key

Words are placed backwards, forward, diagonally, up and down. Words listed below are included in the maze. Circle the hidden vocabulary words in the maze.

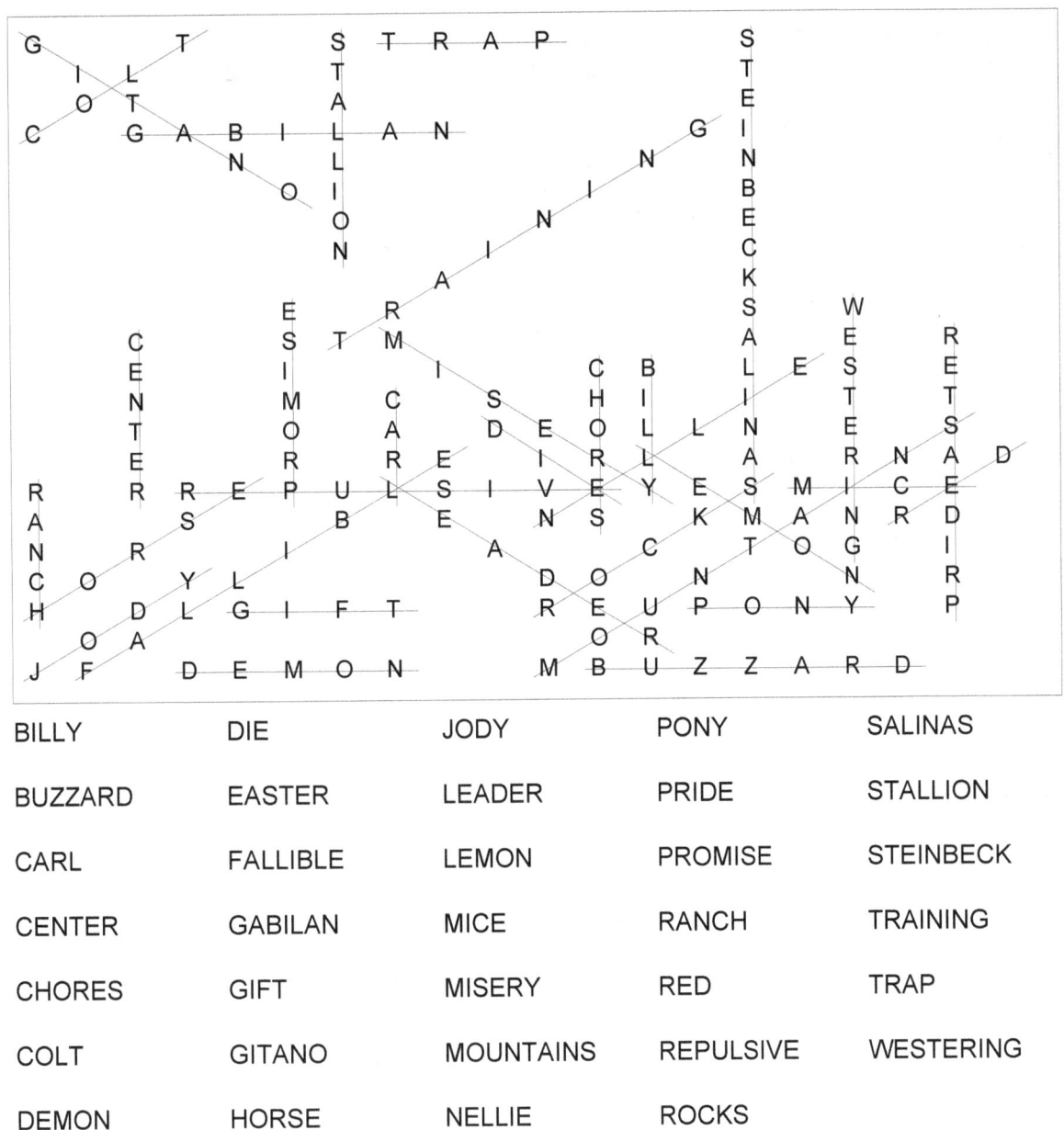

BILLY	DIE	JODY	PONY	SALINAS
BUZZARD	EASTER	LEADER	PRIDE	STALLION
CARL	FALLIBLE	LEMON	PROMISE	STEINBECK
CENTER	GABILAN	MICE	RANCH	TRAINING
CHORES	GIFT	MISERY	RED	TRAP
COLT	GITANO	MOUNTAINS	REPULSIVE	WESTERING
DEMON	HORSE	NELLIE	ROCKS	

Red Pony Word Search 4

Words are placed backwards, forward, diagonally, up and down. Words listed below are included in the maze. Circle the hidden vocabulary words in the maze.

```
T W C N Y L L D S A L I N A S L E M O N
R N E E P J L E G V Y G M N N Z R G Q
A M N L X R T S A M H X N S I T X E W L
P C T L F M P G J D O T Q L A C G P R G
Y B E I F C B V V D E N L C T F R U G H
N F R E S K Z N K C L R B B N S V L N V
W S G C Q N N Y P T Y N T Y U F S S C J
K W N J L Y Y X Y P P Z K K O G N I N T
G T B M M P T Q P Y S L D N M N J V S W
V M P G K V P Z V H Z T Y H A C K E S N
J P I C P Z P R K D F F E L F W P K K V
X H V S G S K Y P P Q Q I I G J R Q M P
B F L P E E M V O R C B H D N P I F I X
K W G G R R J N Z S A A O D S B D N C G
G I T A N O Y V J G N I R E T S E W E V
N L T M D H M X N B D A S L Q T I C H L
Y H Z Y N C V I M Z E E B V A D T K V
H F W S Q P N J S Z C A H I F L C F V W
R O C K S I M G U E O S S L Y L L I B V
X J V X A G W B V B L T G L G I Q G D D
T C D R C X J Z X P T E Q A M O R G E W
L J T R A N C H R S B R V F K N R R Z N
```

BILLY	DIE	JODY	PONY	SALINAS
BUZZARD	EASTER	LEADER	PRIDE	STALLION
CARL	FALLIBLE	LEMON	PROMISE	STEINBECK
CENTER	GABILAN	MICE	RANCH	TRAINING
CHORES	GIFT	MISERY	RED	TRAP
COLT	GITANO	MOUNTAINS	REPULSIVE	WESTERING
DEMON	HORSE	NELLIE	ROCKS	

Red Pony Word Search 4 Answer Key

Words are placed backwards, forward, diagonally, up and down. Words listed below are included in the maze. Circle the hidden vocabulary words in the maze.

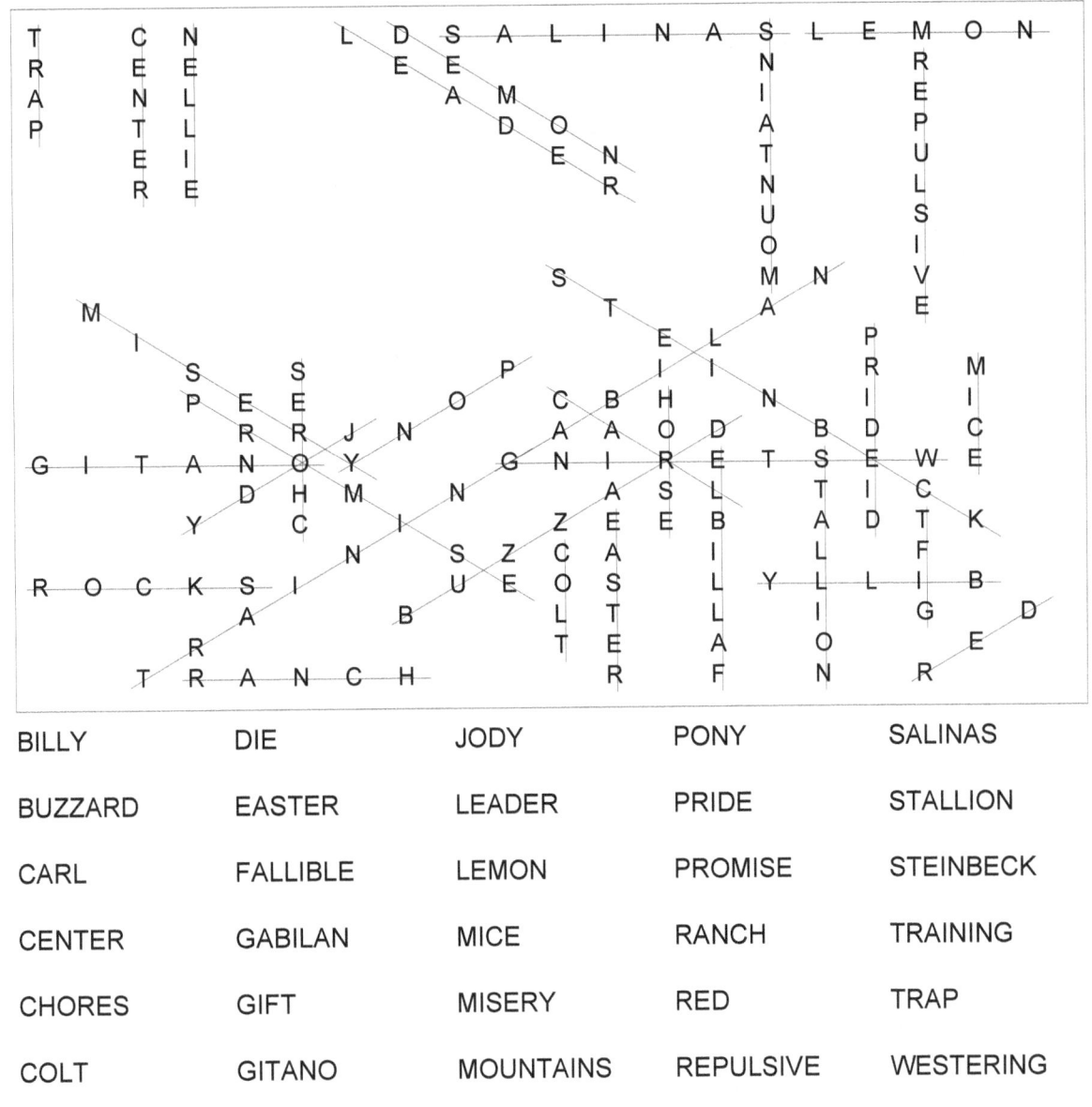

BILLY	DIE	JODY	PONY	SALINAS
BUZZARD	EASTER	LEADER	PRIDE	STALLION
CARL	FALLIBLE	LEMON	PROMISE	STEINBECK
CENTER	GABILAN	MICE	RANCH	TRAINING
CHORES	GIFT	MISERY	RED	TRAP
COLT	GITANO	MOUNTAINS	REPULSIVE	WESTERING
DEMON	HORSE	NELLIE	ROCKS	

Red Pony Crossword 1

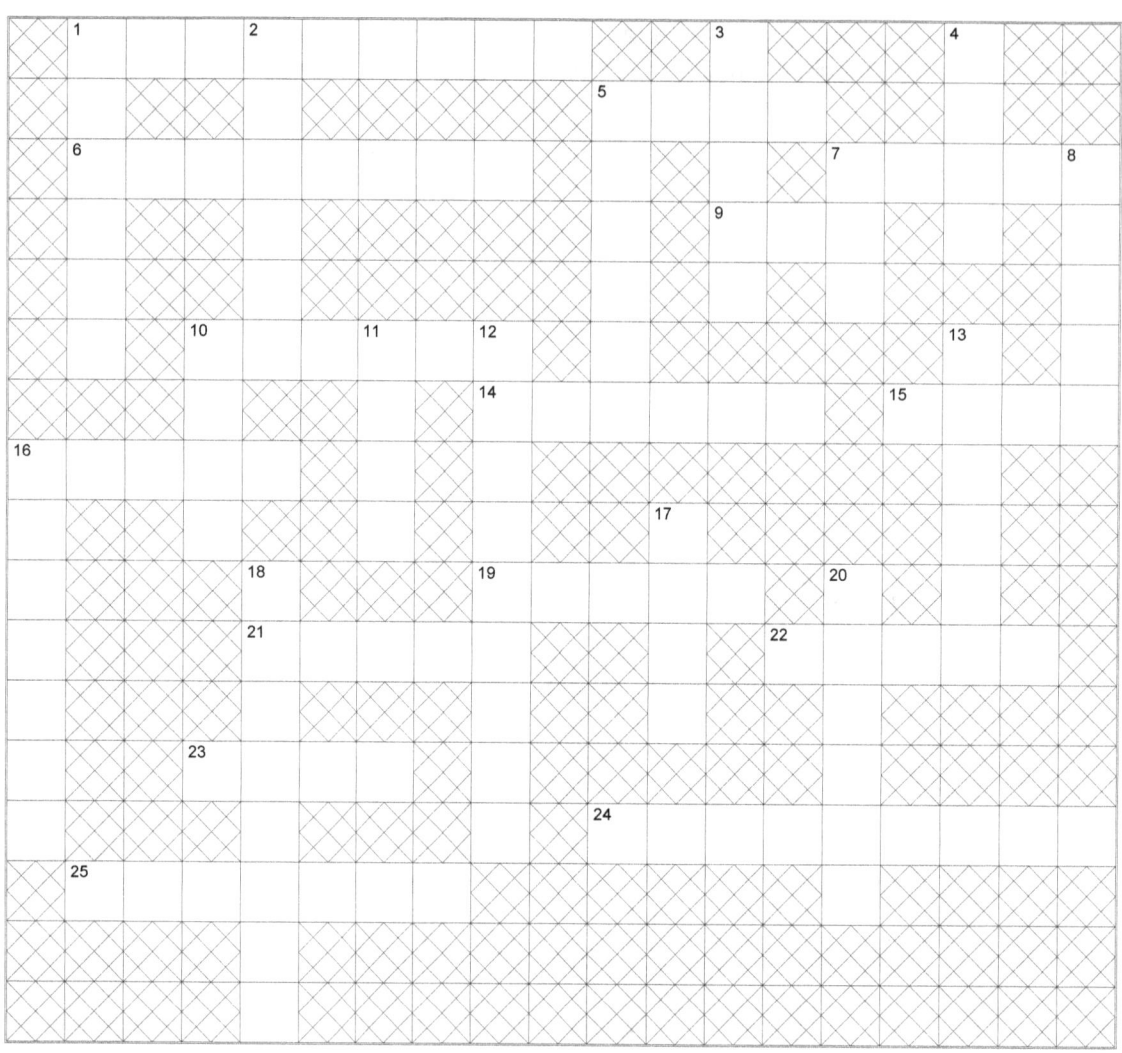

Across
1. Section II: The Great ____
5. Jody's father
6. Male horse
7. Place where Billy Buck works
9. Gitano came home to do this
10. The brush line where there was a patch of perpetually green grass was Jody's ____ point
14. Carl's old horse
15. Jody kills ____ in the haystack
16. ____ Buck; ranch hand
19. Jody asked for only one
21. Jody threw them at birds
22. Black ____; the colt
23. Section I: The ____
24. It has died out of the people
25. The red pony

Down
1. Old things ought to be put out of their ____
2. Mare who died berthing
3. Mrs. Tiflin felt 'a curious ____ rise up in her'
4. The Red ____
5. Jobs Jody had to do on the ranch
7. Color of the pony
8. Easter, for example
10. Baby horse
11. Jody snapped a dog's nose in one
12. The black cypress tree where pigs were slaughtered was ____ to Jody
13. Mexican man who came home to die
16. Jody beat it to death
17. He got a pony
18. The red pony resented ____
20. Section IV: The ____ of the People

Red Pony Crossword 1 Answer Key

		1 M	O	U	2 N	T	A	I	N	S			3 P			4 P	
		I			E					5 C	A	R	L			O	
		6 S	T	A	L	L	I	O	N				I		7 R	A	N	8 H
		E			L					H			9 D	I	E		Y	O
		R			I					O			E		D			R
		Y		10 C	E	11 N	T	12 R		E				13 G			S
				O		R		14 E	A	S	T	E	R	15 M	I	C	E
16 B	I	L	L	Y		A		P				17 J		T		
U				T		P		U				J		A		
Z				18 T		19 L	E	M	O	N		20 L		N		
Z				21 R	O	C	K	S		D		22 D	E	M	O	N
A				A				I		Y		A				
R			23 G	I	F	T		V				D				
D			I				24 E	W	E	S	T	E	R	I	N	G
	25 G	A	B	I	L	A	N					R				
			N													
			G													

Across
1. Section II: The Great ____
5. Jody's father
6. Male horse
7. Place where Billy Buck works
9. Gitano came home to do this
10. The brush line where there was a patch of perpetually green grass was Jody's ____ point
14. Carl's old horse
15. Jody kills ____ in the haystack
16. ____ Buck; ranch hand
19. Jody asked for only one
21. Jody threw them at birds
22. Black ____; the colt
23. Section I: The ____
24. It has died out of the people
25. The red pony

Down
1. Old things ought to be put out of their ___
2. Mare who died berthing
3. Mrs. Tiflin felt 'a curious ____ rise up in her'
4. The Red ____
5. Jobs Jody had to do on the ranch
7. Color of the pony
8. Easter, for example
10. Baby horse
11. Jody snapped a dog's nose in one
12. The black cypress tree where pigs were slaughtered was ____ to Jody
13. Mexican man who came home to die
16. Jody beat it to death
17. He got a pony
18. The red pony resented ____
20. Section IV: The ____ of the People

Red Pony Crossword 2

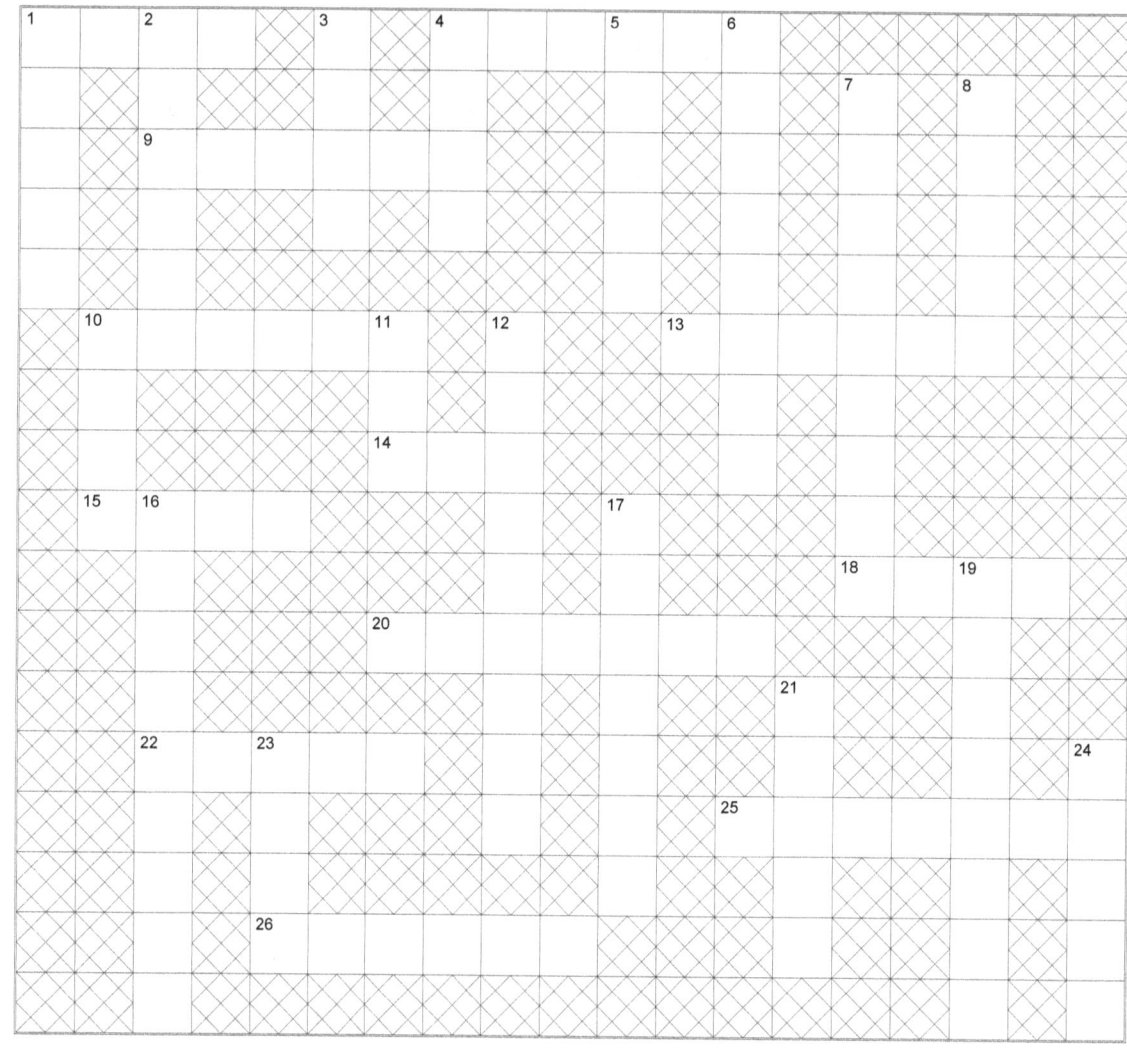

Across
1. The Red ____
4. Jobs Jody had to do on the ranch
9. Section IV: The ____ of the People
10. The brush line where there was a patch of perpetually green grass was Jody's ____ point
13. Old things ought to be put out of their ___
14. Gitano came home to do this
15. Jody snapped a dog's nose in one
18. Section I: The ____
20. The red pony
22. Jody asked for only one
25. Section III: The ____
26. Carl's old horse

Down
1. Mrs. Tiflin felt 'a curious ____ rise up in her'
2. Mare who died berthing
3. He got a pony
4. Jody's father
5. Place where Billy Buck works
6. Male horse
7. It has died out of the people
8. ____ Buck; ranch hand
10. Baby horse
11. Color of the pony
12. Author
16. The black cypress tree where pigs were slaughtered was ____ to Jody
17. Mr. Tiflin sold cows & bought a pony there
19. Billy looked away....He had no right to be ____
21. Easter, for example
23. Jody kills ____ in the haystack
24. Black ____; the colt

Red Pony Crossword 2 Answer Key

	1 P	2 O	N	Y		3 J		4 C	H	5 O	R	6 E	S			
	R		E			O		A		A		T		7 W		8 B
	I		9 L	E	A	D	E	R		N		A		E		I
	D		L			Y		L		C		L		S		L
	E		I							H		L		T		L
		10 C	E	N	T	11 E	R	12 S		13 M	I	S	E	R	Y	
		O				E		T				O		R		
		L				14 D	I	E				N		I		
	15 T	16 R	A	P				I		17 S		N				
		E						N		A				18 G	I	19 F	T
		P				20 G	A	B	I	L	A	N				A
		U				E		I			21 H					L
		22 L	E	23 M	O	N		C		N		O				L	24 D
		S		I				K		A		25 P	R	O	M	I	S	E
		I		C				A		S		S		B		M
		V		26 E	A	S	T	E	R			E		L		O
		E												E		N

Across
1. The Red ____
4. Jobs Jody had to do on the ranch
9. Section IV: The ____ of the People
10. The brush line where there was a patch of perpetually green grass was Jody's ____ point
13. Old things ought to be put out of their ___
14. Gitano came home to do this
15. Jody snapped a dog's nose in one
18. Section I: The ____
20. The red pony
22. Jody asked for only one
25. Section III: The ____
26. Carl's old horse

Down
1. Mrs. Tiflin felt 'a curious ____ rise up in her'
2. Mare who died berthing
3. He got a pony
4. Jody's father
5. Place where Billy Buck works
6. Male horse
7. It has died out of the people
8. ____ Buck; ranch hand
10. Baby horse
11. Color of the pony
12. Author
16. The black cypress tree where pigs were slaughtered was ____ to Jody
17. Mr. Tiflin sold cows & bought a pony there
19. Billy looked away....He had no right to be ____
21. Easter, for example
23. Jody kills ____ in the haystack
24. Black ____; the colt

Red Pony Crossword 3

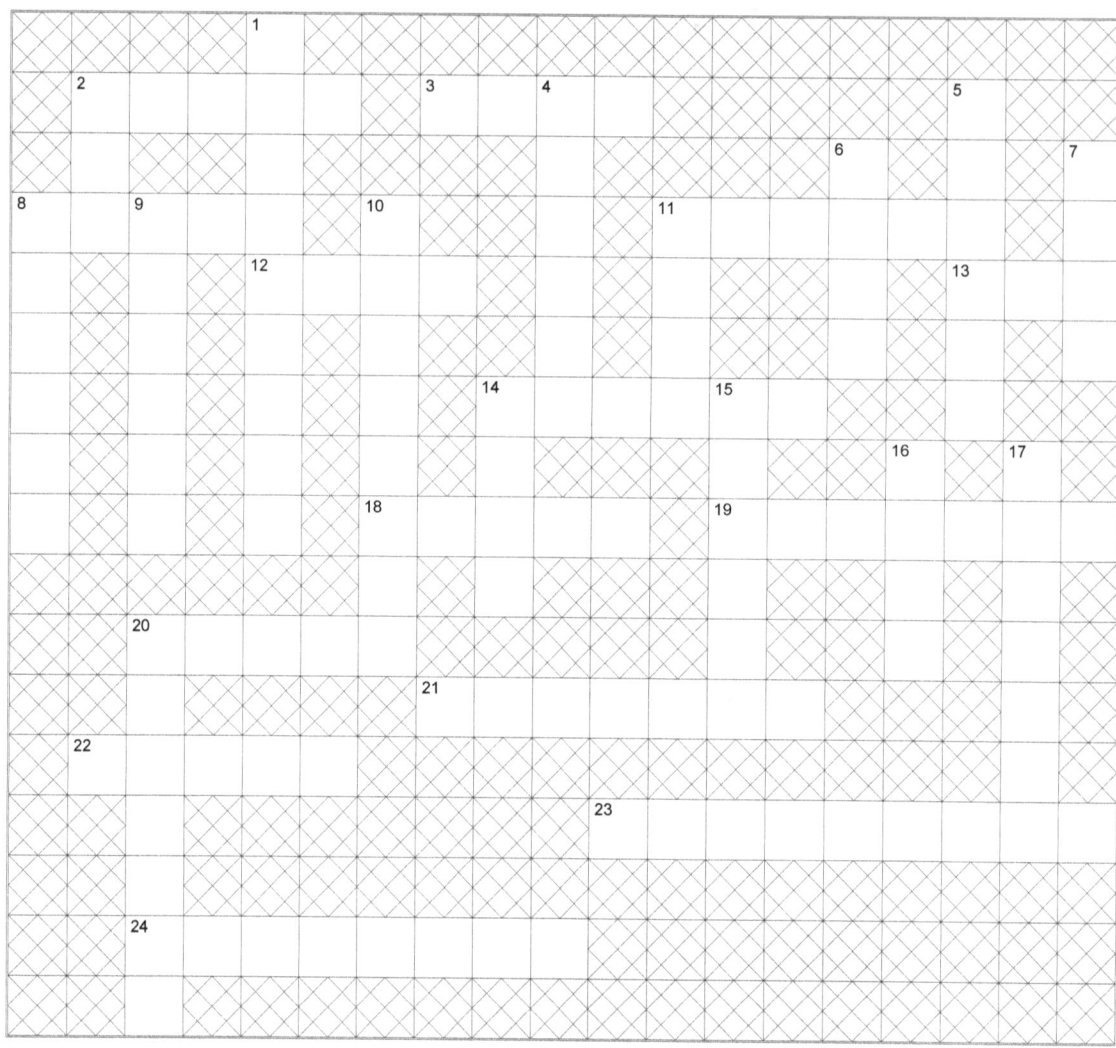

Across

2. Black ____; the colt
3. The Red ____
8. Jody asked for only one
11. Mexican man who came home to die
12. Jody snapped a dog's nose in one
13. Color of the pony
14. The brush line where there was a patch of perpetually green grass was Jody's ____ point
18. ____ Buck; ranch hand
19. Mr. Tiflin sold cows & bought a pony there
20. Mrs. Tiflin felt 'a curious ____ rise up in her'
21. Jody beat it to death
22. Jody threw them at birds
23. It has died out of the people
24. Male horse

Down

1. Section II: The Great ____
2. Gitano came home to do this
4. Mare who died berthing
5. Jobs Jody had to do on the ranch
6. Jody's father
7. He got a pony
8. Section IV: The ____ of the People
9. Old things ought to be put out of their ___
10. Billy looked away....He had no right to be ____
11. Section I: The ____
14. Baby horse
15. Carl's old horse
16. Jody kills ____ in the haystack
17. The red pony
20. Section III: The ____

Red Pony Crossword 3 Answer Key

				1 M								
	2 D	E	M	O	N		3 P	O	4 N	Y		5 C
		I		U					E		6 C	H	7 J
8 L	9 M	O	N		10 F			11 G	I	T	A	N	O	O
	E				12 T	R	A	P		L		I		R	13 R	E	D
	A		S		A		L			I		F		L		E		Y
	D		E		I		L		14 C	E	N	T	15 E	R		S		
	E		R		N		I		O				A		16 M		17 G	
	R		Y		S		18 B	I	L	L	Y		19 S	A	L	I	N	A	S
					L		T				T		C		B	
		20 P	R	I	D	E				E		E		I	
		R			21 B	U	Z	Z	A	R	D			L	
	22 R	O	C	K	S								A	
		M					23 W	E	S	T	E	R	I	N	G
		I											
	24 S	T	A	L	L	I	O	N					
		E											

Across
2. Black ____; the colt
3. The Red ____
8. Jody asked for only one
11. Mexican man who came home to die
12. Jody snapped a dog's nose in one
13. Color of the pony
14. The brush line where there was a patch of perpetually green grass was Jody's ____ point
18. ____ Buck; ranch hand
19. Mr. Tiflin sold cows & bought a pony there
20. Mrs. Tiflin felt 'a curious ____ rise up in her'
21. Jody beat it to death
22. Jody threw them at birds
23. It has died out of the people
24. Male horse

Down
1. Section II: The Great ____
2. Gitano came home to do this
4. Mare who died berthing
5. Jobs Jody had to do on the ranch
6. Jody's father
7. He got a pony
8. Section IV: The ____ of the People
9. Old things ought to be put out of their ____
10. Billy looked away....He had no right to be ____
11. Section I: The ____
14. Baby horse
15. Carl's old horse
16. Jody kills ____ in the haystack
17. The red pony
20. Section III: The ____

41
Copyrighted

Red Pony Crossword 4

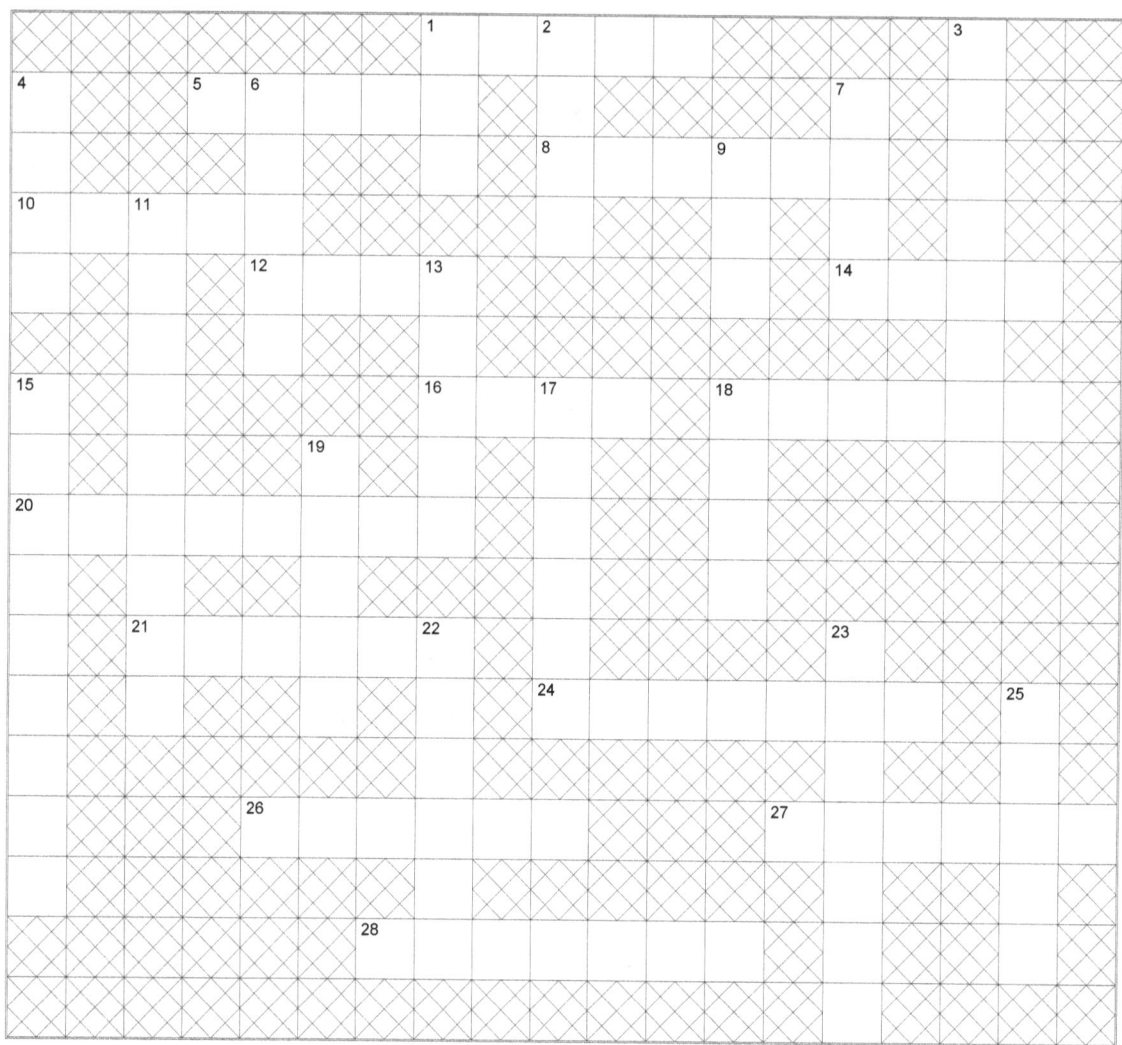

Across
1. Jody threw them at birds
5. Mrs. Tiflin felt 'a curious ____ rise up in her'
8. Section IV: The ____ of the People
10. Black ____; the colt
12. Jody's father
14. The Red ____
16. Jody kills ____ in the haystack
18. Mexican man who came home to die
20. Male horse
21. Mare who died berthing
24. Mr. Tiflin sold cows & bought a pony there
26. The brush line where there was a patch of perpetually green grass was Jody's ____ point
27. Old things ought to be put out of their ___
28. Section III: The ____

Down
1. Color of the pony
2. Baby horse
3. The red pony resented ____
4. He got a pony
6. Place where Billy Buck works
7. Jody snapped a dog's nose in one
9. Gitano came home to do this
11. Section II: The Great ____
13. Jody asked for only one
15. It has died out of the people
17. Jobs Jody had to do on the ranch
18. Section I: The ____
19. ____ Buck; ranch hand
22. Carl's old horse
23. The red pony
25. Easter, for example

Red Pony Crossword 4 Answer Key

Across
1. Jody threw them at birds
5. Mrs. Tiflin felt 'a curious ____ rise up in her'
8. Section IV: The ____ of the People
10. Black ____; the colt
12. Jody's father
14. The Red ____
16. Jody kills ____ in the haystack
18. Mexican man who came home to die
20. Male horse
21. Mare who died berthing
24. Mr. Tiflin sold cows & bought a pony there
26. The brush line where there was a patch of perpetually green grass was Jody's ____ point
27. Old things ought to be put out of their ___
28. Section III: The ____

Down
1. Color of the pony
2. Baby horse
3. The red pony resented ____
4. He got a pony
6. Place where Billy Buck works
7. Jody snapped a dog's nose in one
9. Gitano came home to do this
11. Section II: The Great ____
13. Jody asked for only one
15. It has died out of the people
17. Jobs Jody had to do on the ranch
18. Section I: The ____
19. ____ Buck; ranch hand
22. Carl's old horse
23. The red pony
25. Easter, for example

Red Pony

STEINBECK	DIE	NELLIE	FALLIBLE	MOUNTAINS
EASTER	DEMON	MISERY	TRAINING	PONY
CENTER	REPULSIVE	FREE SPACE	TRAP	LEADER
RANCH	MICE	COLT	BILLY	LEMON
GABILAN	BUZZARD	CHORES	PRIDE	SALINAS

Red Pony

STALLION	RED	ROCKS	CARL	HORSE
GITANO	WESTERING	PROMISE	JODY	SALINAS
PRIDE	CHORES	FREE SPACE	GABILAN	LEMON
BILLY	COLT	MICE	RANCH	LEADER
TRAP	GIFT	REPULSIVE	CENTER	PONY

Red Pony

MOUNTAINS	TRAINING	STALLION	CARL	GITANO
SALINAS	STEINBECK	RED	DEMON	MICE
JODY	REPULSIVE	FREE SPACE	COLT	DIE
RANCH	FALLIBLE	GIFT	HORSE	CENTER
GABILAN	ROCKS	TRAP	EASTER	WESTERING

Red Pony

PROMISE	LEADER	PRIDE	NELLIE	MISERY
PONY	CHORES	BILLY	LEMON	WESTERING
EASTER	TRAP	FREE SPACE	GABILAN	CENTER
HORSE	GIFT	FALLIBLE	RANCH	DIE
COLT	BUZZARD	REPULSIVE	JODY	MICE

Red Pony

GABILAN	PONY	EASTER	NELLIE	CENTER
LEMON	FALLIBLE	COLT	PROMISE	JODY
BUZZARD	RANCH	FREE SPACE	MISERY	DEMON
TRAP	TRAINING	STALLION	PRIDE	CHORES
CARL	RED	MICE	MOUNTAINS	DIE

Red Pony

GITANO	SALINAS	LEADER	GIFT	WESTERING
STEINBECK	REPULSIVE	HORSE	ROCKS	DIE
MOUNTAINS	MICE	FREE SPACE	CARL	CHORES
PRIDE	STALLION	TRAINING	TRAP	DEMON
MISERY	BILLY	RANCH	BUZZARD	JODY

Red Pony

BILLY	PRIDE	LEMON	CHORES	PONY
DIE	PROMISE	COLT	DEMON	WESTERING
MOUNTAINS	REPULSIVE	FREE SPACE	EASTER	STALLION
CENTER	RANCH	GABILAN	NELLIE	MISERY
BUZZARD	RED	CARL	LEADER	JODY

Red Pony

ROCKS	FALLIBLE	GITANO	TRAP	STEINBECK
TRAINING	GIFT	MICE	HORSE	JODY
LEADER	CARL	FREE SPACE	BUZZARD	MISERY
NELLIE	GABILAN	RANCH	CENTER	STALLION
EASTER	SALINAS	REPULSIVE	MOUNTAINS	WESTERING

Red Pony

FALLIBLE	DEMON	BILLY	MOUNTAINS	CARL
PRIDE	CHORES	STALLION	SALINAS	NELLIE
TRAINING	RANCH	FREE SPACE	ROCKS	WESTERING
PROMISE	TRAP	REPULSIVE	GITANO	GIFT
GABILAN	BUZZARD	MISERY	EASTER	MICE

Red Pony

PONY	COLT	JODY	DIE	LEADER
STEINBECK	HORSE	LEMON	CENTER	MICE
EASTER	MISERY	FREE SPACE	GABILAN	GIFT
GITANO	REPULSIVE	TRAP	PROMISE	WESTERING
ROCKS	RED	RANCH	TRAINING	NELLIE

Red Pony

COLT	CARL	SALINAS	REPULSIVE	WESTERING
JODY	DIE	STALLION	HORSE	MISERY
TRAINING	ROCKS	FREE SPACE	GIFT	PRIDE
BILLY	LEADER	TRAP	EASTER	MICE
RANCH	FALLIBLE	GABILAN	DEMON	CHORES

Red Pony

NELLIE	GITANO	PROMISE	PONY	MOUNTAINS
LEMON	BUZZARD	RED	CENTER	CHORES
DEMON	GABILAN	FREE SPACE	RANCH	MICE
EASTER	TRAP	LEADER	BILLY	PRIDE
GIFT	STEINBECK	ROCKS	TRAINING	MISERY

Red Pony

NELLIE	EASTER	COLT	RANCH	MISERY
HORSE	RED	SALINAS	BUZZARD	PROMISE
STEINBECK	CHORES	FREE SPACE	PRIDE	BILLY
DIE	PONY	CARL	TRAP	GITANO
LEMON	TRAINING	ROCKS	STALLION	FALLIBLE

Red Pony

CENTER	WESTERING	GIFT	MICE	DEMON
JODY	MOUNTAINS	GABILAN	REPULSIVE	FALLIBLE
STALLION	ROCKS	FREE SPACE	LEMON	GITANO
TRAP	CARL	PONY	DIE	BILLY
PRIDE	LEADER	CHORES	STEINBECK	PROMISE

Red Pony

WESTERING	COLT	BILLY	GABILAN	DIE
CHORES	LEADER	GITANO	TRAP	JODY
ROCKS	CENTER	FREE SPACE	MISERY	GIFT
PONY	HORSE	MICE	MOUNTAINS	PROMISE
REPULSIVE	SALINAS	NELLIE	DEMON	BUZZARD

Red Pony

STALLION	LEMON	RANCH	FALLIBLE	CARL
PRIDE	RED	STEINBECK	TRAINING	BUZZARD
DEMON	NELLIE	FREE SPACE	REPULSIVE	PROMISE
MOUNTAINS	MICE	HORSE	PONY	GIFT
MISERY	EASTER	CENTER	ROCKS	JODY

Red Pony

BILLY	FALLIBLE	GABILAN	TRAP	PROMISE
DIE	JODY	GIFT	MISERY	SALINAS
TRAINING	HORSE	FREE SPACE	MICE	ROCKS
EASTER	STALLION	MOUNTAINS	COLT	STEINBECK
CHORES	WESTERING	LEADER	RANCH	RED

Red Pony

REPULSIVE	CARL	DEMON	GITANO	CENTER
PONY	BUZZARD	PRIDE	LEMON	RED
RANCH	LEADER	FREE SPACE	CHORES	STEINBECK
COLT	MOUNTAINS	STALLION	EASTER	ROCKS
MICE	NELLIE	HORSE	TRAINING	SALINAS

Red Pony

STALLION	PRIDE	DEMON	MOUNTAINS	GABILAN
GIFT	WESTERING	TRAP	REPULSIVE	HORSE
CENTER	LEADER	FREE SPACE	CARL	ROCKS
PONY	RED	STEINBECK	GITANO	COLT
BUZZARD	FALLIBLE	JODY	NELLIE	DIE

Red Pony

SALINAS	CHORES	BILLY	EASTER	PROMISE
MICE	RANCH	LEMON	TRAINING	DIE
NELLIE	JODY	FREE SPACE	BUZZARD	COLT
GITANO	STEINBECK	RED	PONY	ROCKS
CARL	MISERY	LEADER	CENTER	HORSE

Red Pony

MOUNTAINS	PROMISE	SALINAS	BILLY	WESTERING
RED	STEINBECK	REPULSIVE	CENTER	PRIDE
ROCKS	NELLIE	FREE SPACE	JODY	DIE
CHORES	LEMON	STALLION	PONY	DEMON
FALLIBLE	LEADER	CARL	EASTER	HORSE

Red Pony

RANCH	TRAINING	GABILAN	GITANO	MISERY
MICE	COLT	BUZZARD	TRAP	HORSE
EASTER	CARL	FREE SPACE	FALLIBLE	DEMON
PONY	STALLION	LEMON	CHORES	DIE
JODY	GIFT	NELLIE	ROCKS	PRIDE

Red Pony

LEADER	WESTERING	BUZZARD	PRIDE	CARL
MICE	REPULSIVE	HORSE	GABILAN	GITANO
FALLIBLE	EASTER	FREE SPACE	MISERY	BILLY
CHORES	LEMON	GIFT	DIE	TRAINING
SALINAS	PONY	RANCH	COLT	STEINBECK

Red Pony

CENTER	JODY	TRAP	NELLIE	RED
MOUNTAINS	PROMISE	STALLION	ROCKS	STEINBECK
COLT	RANCH	FREE SPACE	SALINAS	TRAINING
DIE	GIFT	LEMON	CHORES	BILLY
MISERY	DEMON	EASTER	FALLIBLE	GITANO

Red Pony

EASTER	REPULSIVE	CENTER	RED	TRAP
HORSE	MICE	STEINBECK	FALLIBLE	GITANO
PONY	LEMON	FREE SPACE	PROMISE	JODY
NELLIE	PRIDE	COLT	RANCH	STALLION
ROCKS	DEMON	SALINAS	GABILAN	WESTERING

Red Pony

LEADER	CHORES	DIE	MOUNTAINS	GIFT
BILLY	BUZZARD	TRAINING	CARL	WESTERING
GABILAN	SALINAS	FREE SPACE	ROCKS	STALLION
RANCH	COLT	PRIDE	NELLIE	JODY
PROMISE	MISERY	LEMON	PONY	GITANO

Red Pony

MOUNTAINS	GITANO	CHORES	PONY	DEMON
ROCKS	GABILAN	RED	BILLY	JODY
GIFT	DIE	FREE SPACE	CENTER	PROMISE
HORSE	COLT	TRAP	MICE	WESTERING
FALLIBLE	EASTER	BUZZARD	STEINBECK	TRAINING

Red Pony

MISERY	LEMON	CARL	REPULSIVE	NELLIE
LEADER	PRIDE	RANCH	STALLION	TRAINING
STEINBECK	BUZZARD	FREE SPACE	FALLIBLE	WESTERING
MICE	TRAP	COLT	HORSE	PROMISE
CENTER	SALINAS	DIE	GIFT	JODY

Red Pony

BUZZARD	STEINBECK	DIE	CARL	LEMON
JODY	MOUNTAINS	RED	GIFT	PROMISE
GITANO	GABILAN	FREE SPACE	PONY	ROCKS
LEADER	TRAP	STALLION	PRIDE	REPULSIVE
DEMON	MISERY	BILLY	MICE	CHORES

Red Pony

HORSE	SALINAS	WESTERING	CENTER	TRAINING
FALLIBLE	EASTER	NELLIE	COLT	CHORES
MICE	BILLY	FREE SPACE	DEMON	REPULSIVE
PRIDE	STALLION	TRAP	LEADER	ROCKS
PONY	RANCH	GABILAN	GITANO	PROMISE

Red Pony

EASTER	HORSE	NELLIE	LEMON	TRAINING
MISERY	MOUNTAINS	CARL	DIE	COLT
STEINBECK	GABILAN	FREE SPACE	WESTERING	RANCH
LEADER	GITANO	PROMISE	GIFT	PONY
DEMON	BILLY	CENTER	PRIDE	STALLION

Red Pony

TRAP	FALLIBLE	SALINAS	MICE	CHORES
JODY	BUZZARD	RED	ROCKS	STALLION
PRIDE	CENTER	FREE SPACE	DEMON	PONY
GIFT	PROMISE	GITANO	LEADER	RANCH
WESTERING	REPULSIVE	GABILAN	STEINBECK	COLT

Red Pony Vocabulary Word List

No.	Word	Clue/Definition
1.	ABRUPTLY	Suddenly
2.	ALOOF	Distant; indifferent; apart
3.	ARROGANT	Haughty; contemptuous; overbearing
4.	COMPLACENT	Self-satisfied; contented
5.	CONSTRUED	Explained; interpreted
6.	CONTEMPLATIVE	Thoughtful; meditative
7.	CONTEMPTUOUSLY	Disdainfully; scornfully
8.	CONVENED	Assembled; came together
9.	DISCONSOLATELY	Sorrowfully; dejectedly
10.	DISPARAGINGLY	Belittlingly; reducing in esteem
11.	DRONED	Made a low, dull, monotonous sound
12.	ELIMINATED	Gotten rid of; left out of consideration
13.	HAMPERED	Prevented action or progress; impeded
14.	IMPERTURBABILITY	Characteristic of not capable of being upset
15.	INCENSED	Enraged; angered
16.	INTRICATELY	With complexly arranged elements
17.	LANGUOROUS	Still; sluggish; listless
18.	LISTLESSLY	Indifferently; unenthusiastically
19.	MARTIALLY	In a military or warlike manner
20.	NONCHALANCE	With a lack of concern; showing indifference
21.	OMINOUSLY	Threateningly
22.	PARALLEL	Equal distance apart at all points; a comparison indicating similarities
23.	PATERNALLY	In a fatherly manner
24.	PERPETUALLY	Continually
25.	PHANTOM	An image that appears only in the mind; ghost
26.	PITEOUSLY	Moving to sympathy
27.	POTENTIAL	Latent; possible but not yet so
28.	PRESTIGE	Renown; power to command admiration
29.	RAMBUNCTIOUSNESS	Boisterousness; rowdiness
30.	RETRACT	Take back; withdraw
31.	STAUNCHNESS	Steadfastness; resoluteness
32.	STRENUOUSLY	Energetically; vigorously; actively
33.	VICINITY	Locality; proximity; neighborhood
34.	WHETTED	Sharpened

Red Pony Vocabulary Fill In The Blanks 1

_____ 1. Sorrowfully; dejectedly

_____ 2. Explained; interpreted

_____ 3. With a lack of concern; showing indifference

_____ 4. Enraged; angered

_____ 5. Continually

_____ 6. Haughty; contemptuous; overbearing

_____ 7. Distant; indifferent; apart

_____ 8. Gotten rid of; left out of consideration

_____ 9. Thoughtful; meditative

_____ 10. Renown; power to command admiration

_____ 11. Belittlingly; reducing in esteem

_____ 12. With complexly arranged elements

_____ 13. Assembled; came together

_____ 14. Disdainfully; scornfully

_____ 15. Suddenly

_____ 16. Energetically; vigorously; actively

_____ 17. Locality; proximity; neighborhood

_____ 18. Made a low, dull, monotonous sound

_____ 19. In a military or warlike manner

_____ 20. Characteristic of not capable of being upset

Red Pony Vocabulary Fill In The Blanks 1 Answer Key

DISCONSOLATELY	1. Sorrowfully; dejectedly
CONSTRUED	2. Explained; interpreted
NONCHALANCE	3. With a lack of concern; showing indifference
INCENSED	4. Enraged; angered
PERPETUALLY	5. Continually
ARROGANT	6. Haughty; contemptuous; overbearing
ALOOF	7. Distant; indifferent; apart
ELIMINATED	8. Gotten rid of; left out of consideration
CONTEMPLATIVE	9. Thoughtful; meditative
PRESTIGE	10. Renown; power to command admiration
DISPARAGINGLY	11. Belittlingly; reducing in esteem
INTRICATELY	12. With complexly arranged elements
CONVENED	13. Assembled; came together
CONTEMPTUOUSLY	14. Disdainfully; scornfully
ABRUPTLY	15. Suddenly
STRENUOUSLY	16. Energetically; vigorously; actively
VICINITY	17. Locality; proximity; neighborhood
DRONED	18. Made a low, dull, monotonous sound
MARTIALLY	19. In a military or warlike manner
IMPERTURBABILITY	20. Characteristic of not capable of being upset

Red Pony Vocabulary Fill In The Blanks 2

_____ 1. Indifferently; unenthusiastically

_____ 2. Haughty; contemptuous; overbearing

_____ 3. With complexly arranged elements

_____ 4. Energetically; vigorously; actively

_____ 5. Steadfastness; resoluteness

_____ 6. Assembled; came together

_____ 7. Thoughtful; meditative

_____ 8. Boisterousness; rowdiness

_____ 9. With a lack of concern; showing indifference

_____ 10. Take back; withdraw

_____ 11. Moving to sympathy

_____ 12. Prevented action or progress; impeded

_____ 13. Enraged; angered

_____ 14. Suddenly

_____ 15. Gotten rid of; left out of consideration

_____ 16. Self-satisfied; contented

_____ 17. Equal distance apart at all points; a comparison indicating similarities

_____ 18. Still; sluggish; listless

_____ 19. An image that appears only in the mind; ghost

_____ 20. Made a low, dull, monotonous sound

Red Pony Vocabulary Fill In The Blanks 2 Answer Key

LISTLESSLY	1. Indifferently; unenthusiastically
ARROGANT	2. Haughty; contemptuous; overbearing
INTRICATELY	3. With complexly arranged elements
STRENUOUSLY	4. Energetically; vigorously; actively
STAUNCHNESS	5. Steadfastness; resoluteness
CONVENED	6. Assembled; came together
CONTEMPLATIVE	7. Thoughtful; meditative
RAMBUNCTIOUSNESS	8. Boisterousness; rowdiness
NONCHALANCE	9. With a lack of concern; showing indifference
RETRACT	10. Take back; withdraw
PITEOUSLY	11. Moving to sympathy
HAMPERED	12. Prevented action or progress; impeded
INCENSED	13. Enraged; angered
ABRUPTLY	14. Suddenly
ELIMINATED	15. Gotten rid of; left out of consideration
COMPLACENT	16. Self-satisfied; contented
PARALLEL	17. Equal distance apart at all points; a comparison indicating similarities
LANGUOROUS	18. Still; sluggish; listless
PHANTOM	19. An image that appears only in the mind; ghost
DRONED	20. Made a low, dull, monotonous sound

Red Pony Vocabulary Fill In The Blanks 3

_____ 1. Continually

_____ 2. Moving to sympathy

_____ 3. Suddenly

_____ 4. Belittlingly; reducing in esteem

_____ 5. Indifferently; unenthusiastically

_____ 6. Boisterousness; rowdiness

_____ 7. Disdainfully; scornfully

_____ 8. Sorrowfully; dejectedly

_____ 9. Renown; power to command admiration

_____ 10. Still; sluggish; listless

_____ 11. Take back; withdraw

_____ 12. Explained; interpreted

_____ 13. Assembled; came together

_____ 14. Equal distance apart at all points; a comparison indicating similarities

_____ 15. Latent; possible but not yet so

_____ 16. Self-satisfied; contented

_____ 17. An image that appears only in the mind; ghost

_____ 18. Haughty; contemptuous; overbearing

_____ 19. Energetically; vigorously; actively

_____ 20. With complexly arranged elements

Red Pony Vocabulary Fill In The Blanks 3 Answer Key

PERPETUALLY	1. Continually
PITEOUSLY	2. Moving to sympathy
ABRUPTLY	3. Suddenly
DISPARAGINGLY	4. Belittlingly; reducing in esteem
LISTLESSLY	5. Indifferently; unenthusiastically
RAMBUNCTIOUSNESS	6. Boisterousness; rowdiness
CONTEMPTUOUSLY	7. Disdainfully; scornfully
DISCONSOLATELY	8. Sorrowfully; dejectedly
PRESTIGE	9. Renown; power to command admiration
LANGUOROUS	10. Still; sluggish; listless
RETRACT	11. Take back; withdraw
CONSTRUED	12. Explained; interpreted
CONVENED	13. Assembled; came together
PARALLEL	14. Equal distance apart at all points; a comparison indicating similarities
POTENTIAL	15. Latent; possible but not yet so
COMPLACENT	16. Self-satisfied; contented
PHANTOM	17. An image that appears only in the mind; ghost
ARROGANT	18. Haughty; contemptuous; overbearing
STRENUOUSLY	19. Energetically; vigorously; actively
INTRICATELY	20. With complexly arranged elements

Red Pony Vocabulary Fill In The Blanks 4

1. Sharpened
2. Steadfastness; resoluteness
3. Haughty; contemptuous; overbearing
4. Take back; withdraw
5. Thoughtful; meditative
6. Threateningly
7. Suddenly
8. Disdainfully; scornfully
9. Self-satisfied; contented
10. Indifferently; unenthusiastically
11. Renown; power to command admiration
12. Characteristic of not capable of being upset
13. With complexly arranged elements
14. Energetically; vigorously; actively
15. Continually
16. Explained; interpreted
17. Belittlingly; reducing in esteem
18. Sorrowfully; dejectedly
19. Assembled; came together
20. Still; sluggish; listless

Red Pony Vocabulary Fill In The Blanks 4 Answer Key

WHETTED	1. Sharpened
STAUNCHNESS	2. Steadfastness; resoluteness
ARROGANT	3. Haughty; contemptuous; overbearing
RETRACT	4. Take back; withdraw
CONTEMPLATIVE	5. Thoughtful; meditative
OMINOUSLY	6. Threateningly
ABRUPTLY	7. Suddenly
CONTEMPTUOUSLY	8. Disdainfully; scornfully
COMPLACENT	9. Self-satisfied; contented
LISTLESSLY	10. Indifferently; unenthusiastically
PRESTIGE	11. Renown; power to command admiration
IMPERTURBABILITY	12. Characteristic of not capable of being upset
INTRICATELY	13. With complexly arranged elements
STRENUOUSLY	14. Energetically; vigorously; actively
PERPETUALLY	15. Continually
CONSTRUED	16. Explained; interpreted
DISPARAGINGLY	17. Belittlingly; reducing in esteem
DISCONSOLATELY	18. Sorrowfully; dejectedly
CONVENED	19. Assembled; came together
LANGUOROUS	20. Still; sluggish; listless

Red Pony Vocabulary Matching 1

___ 1. OMINOUSLY   A. Gotten rid of; left out of consideration
___ 2. PERPETUALLY   B. Haughty; contemptuous; overbearing
___ 3. ALOOF   C. Made a low, dull, monotonous sound
___ 4. ARROGANT   D. Self-satisfied; contented
___ 5. CONTEMPLATIVE   E. Prevented action or progress; impeded
___ 6. INCENSED   F. Assembled; came together
___ 7. PITEOUSLY   G. Sorrowfully; dejectedly
___ 8. NONCHALANCE   H. Moving to sympathy
___ 9. WHETTED   I. Sharpened
___10. DISPARAGINGLY   J. In a fatherly manner
___11. HAMPERED   K. Latent; possible but not yet so
___12. MARTIALLY   L. Renown; power to command admiration
___13. ABRUPTLY   M. Enraged; angered
___14. ELIMINATED   N. Steadfastness; resoluteness
___15. CONVENED   O. Characteristic of not capable of being upset
___16. STAUNCHNESS   P. Thoughtful; meditative
___17. COMPLACENT   Q. Suddenly
___18. IMPERTURBABILITY   R. Continually
___19. POTENTIAL   S. Indifferently; unenthusiastically
___20. DISCONSOLATELY   T. Threateningly
___21. PRESTIGE   U. In a military or warlike manner
___22. DRONED   V. With a lack of concern; showing indifference
___23. PATERNALLY   W. Belittlingly; reducing in esteem
___24. LISTLESSLY   X. Locality; proximity; neighborhood
___25. VICINITY   Y. Distant; indifferent; apart

Red Pony Vocabulary Matching 1 Answer Key

T - 1. OMINOUSLY	A. Gotten rid of; left out of consideration
R - 2. PERPETUALLY	B. Haughty; contemptuous; overbearing
Y - 3. ALOOF	C. Made a low, dull, monotonous sound
B - 4. ARROGANT	D. Self-satisfied; contented
P - 5. CONTEMPLATIVE	E. Prevented action or progress; impeded
M - 6. INCENSED	F. Assembled; came together
H - 7. PITEOUSLY	G. Sorrowfully; dejectedly
V - 8. NONCHALANCE	H. Moving to sympathy
I - 9. WHETTED	I. Sharpened
W - 10. DISPARAGINGLY	J. In a fatherly manner
E - 11. HAMPERED	K. Latent; possible but not yet so
U - 12. MARTIALLY	L. Renown; power to command admiration
Q - 13. ABRUPTLY	M. Enraged; angered
A - 14. ELIMINATED	N. Steadfastness; resoluteness
F - 15. CONVENED	O. Characteristic of not capable of being upset
N - 16. STAUNCHNESS	P. Thoughtful; meditative
D - 17. COMPLACENT	Q. Suddenly
O - 18. IMPERTURBABILITY	R. Continually
K - 19. POTENTIAL	S. Indifferently; unenthusiastically
G - 20. DISCONSOLATELY	T. Threateningly
L - 21. PRESTIGE	U. In a military or warlike manner
C - 22. DRONED	V. With a lack of concern; showing indifference
J - 23. PATERNALLY	W. Belittlingly; reducing in esteem
S - 24. LISTLESSLY	X. Locality; proximity; neighborhood
X - 25. VICINITY	Y. Distant; indifferent; apart

Red Pony Vocabulary Matching 2

___ 1. PITEOUSLY
___ 2. CONVENED
___ 3. WHETTED
___ 4. RAMBUNCTIOUSNESS
___ 5. MARTIALLY
___ 6. POTENTIAL
___ 7. INTRICATELY
___ 8. PERPETUALLY
___ 9. HAMPERED
___ 10. PRESTIGE
___ 11. ALOOF
___ 12. CONTEMPLATIVE
___ 13. PHANTOM
___ 14. RETRACT
___ 15. VICINITY
___ 16. COMPLACENT
___ 17. LANGUOROUS
___ 18. STAUNCHNESS
___ 19. OMINOUSLY
___ 20. CONTEMPTUOUSLY
___ 21. PARALLEL
___ 22. CONSTRUED
___ 23. DRONED
___ 24. STRENUOUSLY
___ 25. PATERNALLY

A. Take back; withdraw
B. Prevented action or progress; impeded
C. Assembled; came together
D. Disdainfully; scornfully
E. Locality; proximity; neighborhood
F. An image that appears only in the mind; ghost
G. In a military or warlike manner
H. Equal distance apart at all points; a comparison indicating similarities
I. Boisterousness; rowdiness
J. Made a low, dull, monotonous sound
K. Energetically; vigorously; actively
L. Latent; possible but not yet so
M. Continually
N. With complexly arranged elements
O. Explained; interpreted
P. In a fatherly manner
Q. Still; sluggish; listless
R. Steadfastness; resoluteness
S. Thoughtful; meditative
T. Self-satisfied; contented
U. Distant; indifferent; apart
V. Sharpened
W. Threateningly
X. Moving to sympathy
Y. Renown; power to command admiration

Red Pony Vocabulary Matching 2 Answer Key

X - 1. PITEOUSLY		A. Take back; withdraw
C - 2. CONVENED		B. Prevented action or progress; impeded
V - 3. WHETTED		C. Assembled; came together
I - 4. RAMBUNCTIOUSNESS		D. Disdainfully; scornfully
G - 5. MARTIALLY		E. Locality; proximity; neighborhood
L - 6. POTENTIAL		F. An image that appears only in the mind; ghost
N - 7. INTRICATELY		G. In a military or warlike manner
M - 8. PERPETUALLY		H. Equal distance apart at all points; a comparison indicating similarities
B - 9. HAMPERED		I. Boisterousness; rowdiness
Y - 10. PRESTIGE		J. Made a low, dull, monotonous sound
U - 11. ALOOF		K. Energetically; vigorously; actively
S - 12. CONTEMPLATIVE		L. Latent; possible but not yet so
F - 13. PHANTOM		M. Continually
A - 14. RETRACT		N. With complexly arranged elements
E - 15. VICINITY		O. Explained; interpreted
T - 16. COMPLACENT		P. In a fatherly manner
Q - 17. LANGUOROUS		Q. Still; sluggish; listless
R - 18. STAUNCHNESS		R. Steadfastness; resoluteness
W - 19. OMINOUSLY		S. Thoughtful; meditative
D - 20. CONTEMPTUOUSLY		T. Self-satisfied; contented
H - 21. PARALLEL		U. Distant; indifferent; apart
O - 22. CONSTRUED		V. Sharpened
J - 23. DRONED		W. Threateningly
K - 24. STRENUOUSLY		X. Moving to sympathy
P - 25. PATERNALLY		Y. Renown; power to command admiration

Red Pony Vocabulary Matching 3

___ 1. NONCHALANCE	A. Prevented action or progress; impeded
___ 2. CONVENED	B. With complexly arranged elements
___ 3. POTENTIAL	C. Threateningly
___ 4. DISCONSOLATELY	D. Characteristic of not capable of being upset
___ 5. PHANTOM	E. Explained; interpreted
___ 6. VICINITY	F. Assembled; came together
___ 7. RAMBUNCTIOUSNESS	G. An image that appears only in the mind; ghost
___ 8. CONSTRUED	H. With a lack of concern; showing indifference
___ 9. PERPETUALLY	I. Sorrowfully; dejectedly
___ 10. CONTEMPLATIVE	J. Self-satisfied; contented
___ 11. INTRICATELY	K. Locality; proximity; neighborhood
___ 12. LANGUOROUS	L. Renown; power to command admiration
___ 13. COMPLACENT	M. Moving to sympathy
___ 14. STAUNCHNESS	N. Continually
___ 15. ARROGANT	O. Distant; indifferent; apart
___ 16. STRENUOUSLY	P. Energetically; vigorously; actively
___ 17. PRESTIGE	Q. Boisterousness; rowdiness
___ 18. DISPARAGINGLY	R. Belittlingly; reducing in esteem
___ 19. HAMPERED	S. Haughty; contemptuous; overbearing
___ 20. IMPERTURBABILITY	T. Gotten rid of; left out of consideration
___ 21. ELIMINATED	U. Steadfastness; resoluteness
___ 22. ALOOF	V. Still; sluggish; listless
___ 23. PITEOUSLY	W. Thoughtful; meditative
___ 24. PATERNALLY	X. In a fatherly manner
___ 25. OMINOUSLY	Y. Latent; possible but not yet so

Red Pony Vocabulary Matching 3 Answer Key

H - 1.	NONCHALANCE	A.	Prevented action or progress; impeded
F - 2.	CONVENED	B.	With complexly arranged elements
Y - 3.	POTENTIAL	C.	Threateningly
I - 4.	DISCONSOLATELY	D.	Characteristic of not capable of being upset
G - 5.	PHANTOM	E.	Explained; interpreted
K - 6.	VICINITY	F.	Assembled; came together
Q - 7.	RAMBUNCTIOUSNESS	G.	An image that appears only in the mind; ghost
E - 8.	CONSTRUED	H.	With a lack of concern; showing indifference
N - 9.	PERPETUALLY	I.	Sorrowfully; dejectedly
W - 10.	CONTEMPLATIVE	J.	Self-satisfied; contented
B - 11.	INTRICATELY	K.	Locality; proximity; neighborhood
V - 12.	LANGUOROUS	L.	Renown; power to command admiration
J - 13.	COMPLACENT	M.	Moving to sympathy
U - 14.	STAUNCHNESS	N.	Continually
S - 15.	ARROGANT	O.	Distant; indifferent; apart
P - 16.	STRENUOUSLY	P.	Energetically; vigorously; actively
L - 17.	PRESTIGE	Q.	Boisterousness; rowdiness
R - 18.	DISPARAGINGLY	R.	Belittlingly; reducing in esteem
A - 19.	HAMPERED	S.	Haughty; contemptuous; overbearing
D - 20.	IMPERTURBABILITY	T.	Gotten rid of; left out of consideration
T - 21.	ELIMINATED	U.	Steadfastness; resoluteness
O - 22.	ALOOF	V.	Still; sluggish; listless
M - 23.	PITEOUSLY	W.	Thoughtful; meditative
X - 24.	PATERNALLY	X.	In a fatherly manner
C - 25.	OMINOUSLY	Y.	Latent; possible but not yet so

Red Pony Vocabulary Matching 4

___ 1. CONSTRUED
___ 2. CONTEMPTUOUSLY
___ 3. PERPETUALLY
___ 4. DISPARAGINGLY
___ 5. LISTLESSLY
___ 6. COMPLACENT
___ 7. CONTEMPLATIVE
___ 8. INCENSED
___ 9. RETRACT
___ 10. DISCONSOLATELY
___ 11. HAMPERED
___ 12. LANGUOROUS
___ 13. PITEOUSLY
___ 14. PHANTOM
___ 15. IMPERTURBABILITY
___ 16. CONVENED
___ 17. PRESTIGE
___ 18. MARTIALLY
___ 19. PARALLEL
___ 20. WHETTED
___ 21. VICINITY
___ 22. ELIMINATED
___ 23. ALOOF
___ 24. OMINOUSLY
___ 25. NONCHALANCE

A. Renown; power to command admiration
B. Equal distance apart at all points; a comparison indicating similarities
C. Self-satisfied; contented
D. Disdainfully; scornfully
E. Moving to sympathy
F. In a military or warlike manner
G. Threateningly
H. Indifferently; unenthusiastically
I. Explained; interpreted
J. An image that appears only in the mind; ghost
K. Take back; withdraw
L. Sorrowfully; dejectedly
M. Assembled; came together
N. Gotten rid of; left out of consideration
O. Still; sluggish; listless
P. Locality; proximity; neighborhood
Q. Thoughtful; meditative
R. Belittlingly; reducing in esteem
S. With a lack of concern; showing indifference
T. Sharpened
U. Prevented action or progress; impeded
V. Characteristic of not capable of being upset
W. Enraged; angered
X. Continually
Y. Distant; indifferent; apart

Red Pony Vocabulary Matching 4 Answer Key

I - 1. CONSTRUED		A. Renown; power to command admiration
D - 2. CONTEMPTUOUSLY		B. Equal distance apart at all points; a comparison indicating similarities
X - 3. PERPETUALLY		C. Self-satisfied; contented
R - 4. DISPARAGINGLY		D. Disdainfully; scornfully
H - 5. LISTLESSLY		E. Moving to sympathy
C - 6. COMPLACENT		F. In a military or warlike manner
Q - 7. CONTEMPLATIVE		G. Threateningly
W - 8. INCENSED		H. Indifferently; unenthusiastically
K - 9. RETRACT		I. Explained; interpreted
L - 10. DISCONSOLATELY		J. An image that appears only in the mind; ghost
U - 11. HAMPERED		K. Take back; withdraw
O - 12. LANGUOROUS		L. Sorrowfully; dejectedly
E - 13. PITEOUSLY		M. Assembled; came together
J - 14. PHANTOM		N. Gotten rid of; left out of consideration
V - 15. IMPERTURBABILITY		O. Still; sluggish; listless
M - 16. CONVENED		P. Locality; proximity; neighborhood
A - 17. PRESTIGE		Q. Thoughtful; meditative
F - 18. MARTIALLY		R. Belittlingly; reducing in esteem
B - 19. PARALLEL		S. With a lack of concern; showing indifference
T - 20. WHETTED		T. Sharpened
P - 21. VICINITY		U. Prevented action or progress; impeded
N - 22. ELIMINATED		V. Characteristic of not capable of being upset
Y - 23. ALOOF		W. Enraged; angered
G - 24. OMINOUSLY		X. Continually
S - 25. NONCHALANCE		Y. Distant; indifferent; apart

Red Pony Vocabulary Magic Squares 1

Match the definition with the vocabulary word. Put your answers in the magic squares below. When your answers are correct, all columns and rows will add to the same number.

A. OMINOUSLY
B. PARALLEL
C. DISCONSOLATELY
D. RAMBUNCTIOUSNESS
E. ARROGANT
F. HAMPERED
G. NONCHALANCE
H. ELIMINATED
I. PHANTOM
J. IMPERTURBABILITY
K. COMPLACENT
L. INTRICATELY
M. INCENSED
N. LISTLESSLY
O. ABRUPTLY
P. PERPETUALLY

1. Prevented action or progress; impeded
2. An image that appears only in the mind; ghost
3. Suddenly
4. Boisterousness; rowdiness
5. Enraged; angered
6. Equal distance apart at all points; a comparison indicating similarities
7. Gotten rid of; left out of consideration
8. Self-satisfied; contented
9. Sorrowfully; dejectedly
10. Continually
11. Characteristic of not capable of being upset
12. Haughty; contemptuous; overbearing
13. With complexly arranged elements
14. With a lack of concern; showing indifference
15. Threateningly
16. Indifferently; unenthusiastically

A=	B=	C=	D=
E=	F=	G=	H=
I=	J=	K=	L=
M=	N=	O=	P=

Red Pony Vocabulary Magic Squares 1 Answer Key

Match the definition with the vocabulary word. Put your answers in the magic squares below. When your answers are correct, all columns and rows will add to the same number.

A. OMINOUSLY
B. PARALLEL
C. DISCONSOLATELY
D. RAMBUNCTIOUSNESS
E. ARROGANT
F. HAMPERED
G. NONCHALANCE
H. ELIMINATED
I. PHANTOM
J. IMPERTURBABILITY
K. COMPLACENT
L. INTRICATELY
M. INCENSED
N. LISTLESSLY
O. ABRUPTLY
P. PERPETUALLY

1. Prevented action or progress; impeded
2. An image that appears only in the mind; ghost
3. Suddenly
4. Boisterousness; rowdiness
5. Enraged; angered
6. Equal distance apart at all points; a comparison indicating similarities
7. Gotten rid of; left out of consideration
8. Self-satisfied; contented
9. Sorrowfully; dejectedly
10. Continually
11. Characteristic of not capable of being upset
12. Haughty; contemptuous; overbearing
13. With complexly arranged elements
14. With a lack of concern; showing indifference
15. Threateningly
16. Indifferently; unenthusiastically

A=15	B=6	C=9	D=4
E=12	F=1	G=14	H=7
I=2	J=11	K=8	L=13
M=5	N=16	O=3	P=10

Red Pony Vocabulary Magic Squares 2

Match the definition with the vocabulary word. Put your answers in the magic squares below. When your answers are correct, all columns and rows will add to the same number.

A. ALOOF
B. DISPARAGINGLY
C. DRONED
D. PHANTOM
E. COMPLACENT
F. HAMPERED
G. OMINOUSLY
H. CONTEMPLATIVE
I. NONCHALANCE
J. INCENSED
K. LANGUOROUS
L. PERPETUALLY
M. DISCONSOLATELY
N. RETRACT
O. CONTEMPTUOUSLY
P. ABRUPTLY

1. Disdainfully; scornfully
2. Enraged; angered
3. Thoughtful; meditative
4. Distant; indifferent; apart
5. An image that appears only in the mind; ghost
6. Self-satisfied; contented
7. Still; sluggish; listless
8. Take back; withdraw
9. Prevented action or progress; impeded
10. Made a low, dull, monotonous sound
11. Sorrowfully; dejectedly
12. Continually
13. With a lack of concern; showing indifference
14. Suddenly
15. Belittlingly; reducing in esteem
16. Threateningly

A=	B=	C=	D=
E=	F=	G=	H=
I=	J=	K=	L=
M=	N=	O=	P=

Red Pony Vocabulary Magic Squares 2 Answer Key

Match the definition with the vocabulary word. Put your answers in the magic squares below. When your answers are correct, all columns and rows will add to the same number.

A. ALOOF
B. DISPARAGINGLY
C. DRONED
D. PHANTOM
E. COMPLACENT
F. HAMPERED
G. OMINOUSLY
H. CONTEMPLATIVE
I. NONCHALANCE
J. INCENSED
K. LANGUOROUS
L. PERPETUALLY
M. DISCONSOLATELY
N. RETRACT
O. CONTEMPTUOUSLY
P. ABRUPTLY

1. Disdainfully; scornfully
2. Enraged; angered
3. Thoughtful; meditative
4. Distant; indifferent; apart
5. An image that appears only in the mind; ghost
6. Self-satisfied; contented
7. Still; sluggish; listless
8. Take back; withdraw
9. Prevented action or progress; impeded
10. Made a low, dull, monotonous sound
11. Sorrowfully; dejectedly
12. Continually
13. With a lack of concern; showing indifference
14. Suddenly
15. Belittlingly; reducing in esteem
16. Threateningly

A=4	B=15	C=10	D=5
E=6	F=9	G=16	H=3
I=13	J=2	K=7	L=12
M=11	N=8	O=1	P=14

Red Pony Vocabulary Magic Squares 3

Match the definition with the vocabulary word. Put your answers in the magic squares below. When your answers are correct, all columns and rows will add to the same number.

A. PRESTIGE
B. COMPLACENT
C. WHETTED
D. DISCONSOLATELY
E. PATERNALLY
F. PITEOUSLY
G. MARTIALLY
H. CONVENED
I. INCENSED
J. RETRACT
K. PARALLEL
L. ABRUPTLY
M. LANGUOROUS
N. ARROGANT
O. STAUNCHNESS
P. NONCHALANCE

1. Self-satisfied; contented
2. In a military or warlike manner
3. Equal distance apart at all points; a comparison indicating similarities
4. Haughty; contemptuous; overbearing
5. Still; sluggish; listless
6. Suddenly
7. Assembled; came together
8. Renown; power to command admiration
9. With a lack of concern; showing indifference
10. Enraged; angered
11. In a fatherly manner
12. Sorrowfully; dejectedly
13. Sharpened
14. Moving to sympathy
15. Take back; withdraw
16. Steadfastness; resoluteness

A=	B=	C=	D=
E=	F=	G=	H=
I=	J=	K=	L=
M=	N=	O=	P=

Red Pony Vocabulary Magic Squares 3 Answer Key

Match the definition with the vocabulary word. Put your answers in the magic squares below. When your answers are correct, all columns and rows will add to the same number.

A. PRESTIGE
B. COMPLACENT
C. WHETTED
D. DISCONSOLATELY
E. PATERNALLY
F. PITEOUSLY
G. MARTIALLY
H. CONVENED
I. INCENSED
J. RETRACT
K. PARALLEL
L. ABRUPTLY
M. LANGUOROUS
N. ARROGANT
O. STAUNCHNESS
P. NONCHALANCE

1. Self-satisfied; contented
2. In a military or warlike manner
3. Equal distance apart at all points; a comparison indicating similarities
4. Haughty; contemptuous; overbearing
5. Still; sluggish; listless
6. Suddenly
7. Assembled; came together
8. Renown; power to command admiration
9. With a lack of concern; showing indifference
10. Enraged; angered
11. In a fatherly manner
12. Sorrowfully; dejectedly
13. Sharpened
14. Moving to sympathy
15. Take back; withdraw
16. Steadfastness; resoluteness

A=8	B=1	C=13	D=12
E=11	F=14	G=2	H=7
I=10	J=15	K=3	L=6
M=5	N=4	O=16	P=9

Red Pony Vocabulary Magic Squares 4

Match the definition with the vocabulary word. Put your answers in the magic squares below. When your answers are correct, all columns and rows will add to the same number.

A. STRENUOUSLY
B. PHANTOM
C. DISPARAGINGLY
D. DISCONSOLATELY
E. INCENSED
F. LISTLESSLY
G. PARALLEL
H. STAUNCHNESS
I. ABRUPTLY
J. PATERNALLY
K. ELIMINATED
L. ARROGANT
M. LANGUOROUS
N. PERPETUALLY
O. CONTEMPLATIVE
P. NONCHALANCE

1. Energetically; vigorously; actively
2. Continually
3. In a fatherly manner
4. Enraged; angered
5. Equal distance apart at all points; a comparison indicating similarities
6. Haughty; contemptuous; overbearing
7. With a lack of concern; showing indifference
8. Belittlingly; reducing in esteem
9. Thoughtful; meditative
10. Sorrowfully; dejectedly
11. Steadfastness; resoluteness
12. Gotten rid of; left out of consideration
13. Suddenly
14. Indifferently; unenthusiastically
15. An image that appears only in the mind; ghost
16. Still; sluggish; listless

A=	B=	C=	D=
E=	F=	G=	H=
I=	J=	K=	L=
M=	N=	O=	P=

Red Pony Vocabulary Magic Squares 4 Answer Key

Match the definition with the vocabulary word. Put your answers in the magic squares below. When your answers are correct, all columns and rows will add to the same number.

A. STRENUOUSLY
B. PHANTOM
C. DISPARAGINGLY
D. DISCONSOLATELY
E. INCENSED
F. LISTLESSLY
G. PARALLEL
H. STAUNCHNESS
I. ABRUPTLY
J. PATERNALLY
K. ELIMINATED
L. ARROGANT
M. LANGUOROUS
N. PERPETUALLY
O. CONTEMPLATIVE
P. NONCHALANCE

1. Energetically; vigorously; actively
2. Continually
3. In a fatherly manner
4. Enraged; angered
5. Equal distance apart at all points; a comparison indicating similarities
6. Haughty; contemptuous; overbearing
7. With a lack of concern; showing indifference
8. Belittlingly; reducing in esteem
9. Thoughtful; meditative
10. Sorrowfully; dejectedly
11. Steadfastness; resoluteness
12. Gotten rid of; left out of consideration
13. Suddenly
14. Indifferently; unenthusiastically
15. An image that appears only in the mind; ghost
16. Still; sluggish; listless

A=1	B=15	C=8	D=10
E=4	F=14	G=5	H=11
I=13	J=3	K=12	L=6
M=16	N=2	O=9	P=7

Red Pony Vocabulary Word Search 1

Words are placed backwards, forward, diagonally, up and down. Clues listed below can help you find the words. Circle the hidden vocabulary words in the maze.

```
D I S C O N S O L A T E L Y Y T B C H W
E L I M I N A T E D D E Y L X D B O T L
N L K K F S R J N D L L E L T K N F X
E I P I T E O U S L Y S G T J L Z T F J
V S R P T L L K A R P B N A F T C E H C
N T M T V P D R F H A F I C H Z X M M V
O L C V V F A H V Y T H G I I P T P A F
C E Z N I P Z G T Q E A A R N R N T R D
O S F V O C B F R G R M R T C E A U T R
N S Z T J N I G X R N P A N E S G O I N
T L T G M W C N P F A E P I N T O U A Y
E Y N A Z L M H I M L R S F S I R S L G
M M K H U A A L A T L E I S E G R L L K
P P O M I N O U S L Y D D T D E A Y Y M
L R H P T G C X J M A E F E E U G L R V
A H C O C U Z H K K N N U S T W V T Z P
T Q M F A O C H N O G R C E T D K P R Q
I L X L R R Z X R E T T P E E V T U B Q
V Y O P T O N D B S S R B T H V R R J S
E O J H E U B N N V E S B S W C H B Y J
F R Y T R S D O Z P P O T E N T I A L R
R A M B U N C T I O U S N E S S L N Q N
```

An image that appears only in the mind; ghost (7)
Assembled; came together (8)
Belittlingly; reducing in esteem (13)
Boisterousness; rowdiness (16)
Continually (11)
Disdainfully; scornfully (14)
Distant; indifferent; apart (5)
Enraged; angered (8)
Equal distance apart at all points; a comparison indicating similarities (8)
Explained; interpreted (9)
Gotten rid of; left out of consideration (10)
Haughty; contemptuous; overbearing (8)
In a fatherly manner (10)
In a military or warlike manner (9)
Indifferently; unenthusiastically (10)
Latent; possible but not yet so (9)
Locality; proximity; neighborhood (8)
Made a low, dull, monotonous sound (6)

Moving to sympathy (9)
Prevented action or progress; impeded (8)
Renown; power to command admiration (8)
Sharpened (7)
Sorrowfully; dejectedly (14)
Steadfastness; resoluteness (11)
Still; sluggish; listless (10)
Suddenly (8)
Take back; withdraw (7)
Thoughtful; meditative (13)
Threateningly (9)
With a lack of concern; showing indifference (11)
With complexly arranged elements (11)

Red Pony Vocabulary Word Search 1 Answer Key

Words are placed backwards, forward, diagonally, up and down. Clues listed below can help you find the words. Circle the hidden vocabulary words in the maze.

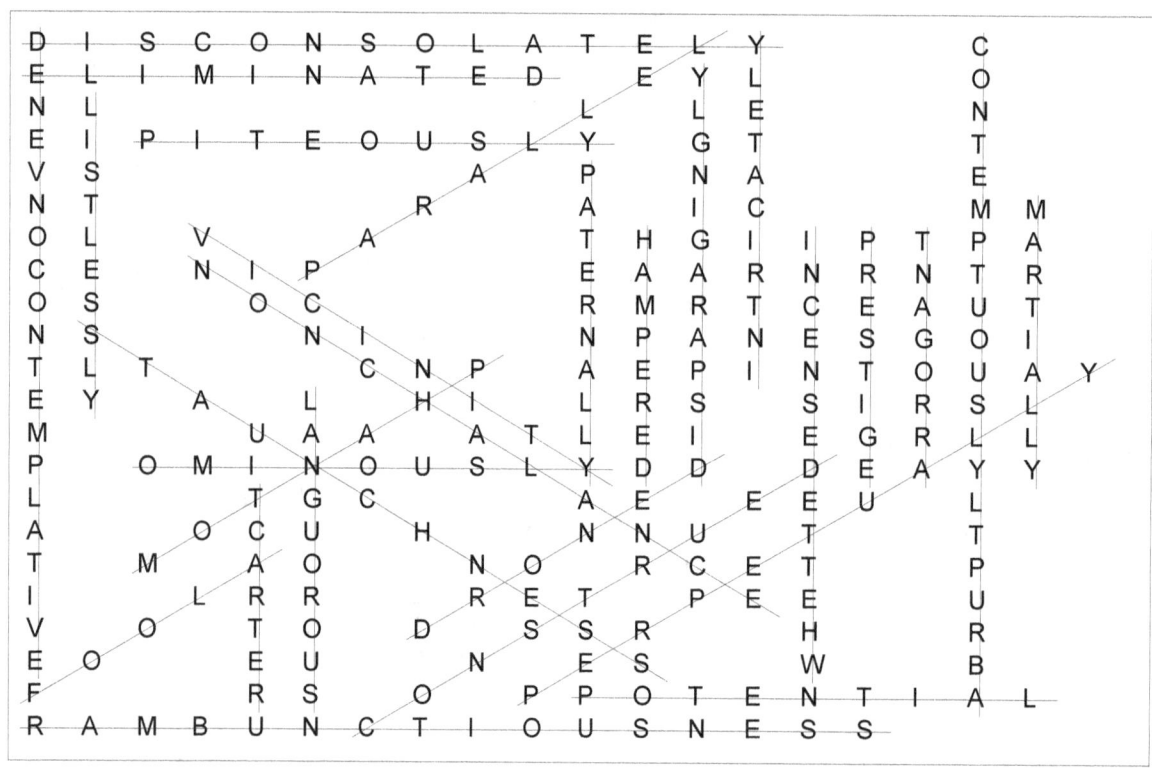

An image that appears only in the mind; ghost (7)
Assembled; came together (8)
Belittlingly; reducing in esteem (13)
Boisterousness; rowdiness (16)
Continually (11)
Disdainfully; scornfully (14)
Distant; indifferent; apart (5)
Enraged; angered (8)
Equal distance apart at all points; a comparison indicating similarities (8)
Explained; interpreted (9)
Gotten rid of; left out of consideration (10)
Haughty; contemptuous; overbearing (8)
In a fatherly manner (10)
In a military or warlike manner (9)
Indifferently; unenthusiastically (10)
Latent; possible but not yet so (9)
Locality; proximity; neighborhood (8)
Made a low, dull, monotonous sound (6)

Moving to sympathy (9)
Prevented action or progress; impeded (8)
Renown; power to command admiration (8)
Sharpened (7)
Sorrowfully; dejectedly (14)
Steadfastness; resoluteness (11)
Still; sluggish; listless (10)
Suddenly (8)
Take back; withdraw (7)
Thoughtful; meditative (13)
Threateningly (9)
With a lack of concern; showing indifference (11)
With complexly arranged elements (11)

Red Pony Vocabulary Word Search 2

Words are placed backwards, forward, diagonally, up and down. Clues listed below can help you find the words. Circle the hidden vocabulary words in the maze.

```
E L I M I N A T E D E N E V N O C O N H
V Y L S U O U T P M E T N O C T I M Q M
H W J M X C C R M Y W S N K C P N I D F
P O T E N T I A L L H C Z F O Y C N Y N
S U O R O U G N A L H G T Z N Y E O I Q
D I S C O N S O L A T E L Y S J N U N S
D C T R K L F G L N R H L W T Q S S T N
Z F B W L X D A A R T K R R Y E L R V
P K N K B Q N D R E Y Y J L U P D Y I L
S A F Q D C E J R T L P M R E Y H W C Y
T V R N E T D V O A L Z P R D L N P A Y
A Y D A T L R K G P A S P G D S N R T V
U S B E L F O R A J I E D P M S C E E V
N Y H B Y L N R N B T E D X D E Y S L L
C W N I M P E R T U R B A B I L I T Y W
H D V B K T D L A E A U V N S T P I T Y
N T Y V R W J L P H M Y P U Q S H G I J
E S B A Z Y L M X D L J O T A I A E N X
S H C N L Y A S H T C E B K L L N X I R
S T Z T X H Z H Q R T T K X O Y T Y C J
M D I S P A R A G I N G L Y O C O T I T
T M T N E C A L P M O C Q N F L M H V V
```

An image that appears only in the mind; ghost (7)
Assembled; came together (8)
Belittlingly; reducing in esteem (13)
Characteristic of not capable of being upset (16)
Continually (11)
Disdainfully; scornfully (14)
Distant; indifferent; apart (5)
Enraged; angered (8)
Equal distance apart at all points; a comparison indicating similarities (8)
Explained; interpreted (9)
Gotten rid of; left out of consideration (10)
Haughty; contemptuous; overbearing (8)
In a fatherly manner (10)
In a military or warlike manner (9)
Indifferently; unenthusiastically (10)
Latent; possible but not yet so (9)
Locality; proximity; neighborhood (8)

Made a low, dull, monotonous sound (6)
Moving to sympathy (9)
Prevented action or progress; impeded (8)
Renown; power to command admiration (8)
Self-satisfied; contented (10)
Sharpened (7)
Sorrowfully; dejectedly (14)
Steadfastness; resoluteness (11)
Still; sluggish; listless (10)
Suddenly (8)
Take back; withdraw (7)
Threateningly (9)
With a lack of concern; showing indifference (11)
With complexly arranged elements (11)

Red Pony Vocabulary Word Search 2 Answer Key

Words are placed backwards, forward, diagonally, up and down. Clues listed below can help you find the words. Circle the hidden vocabulary words in the maze.

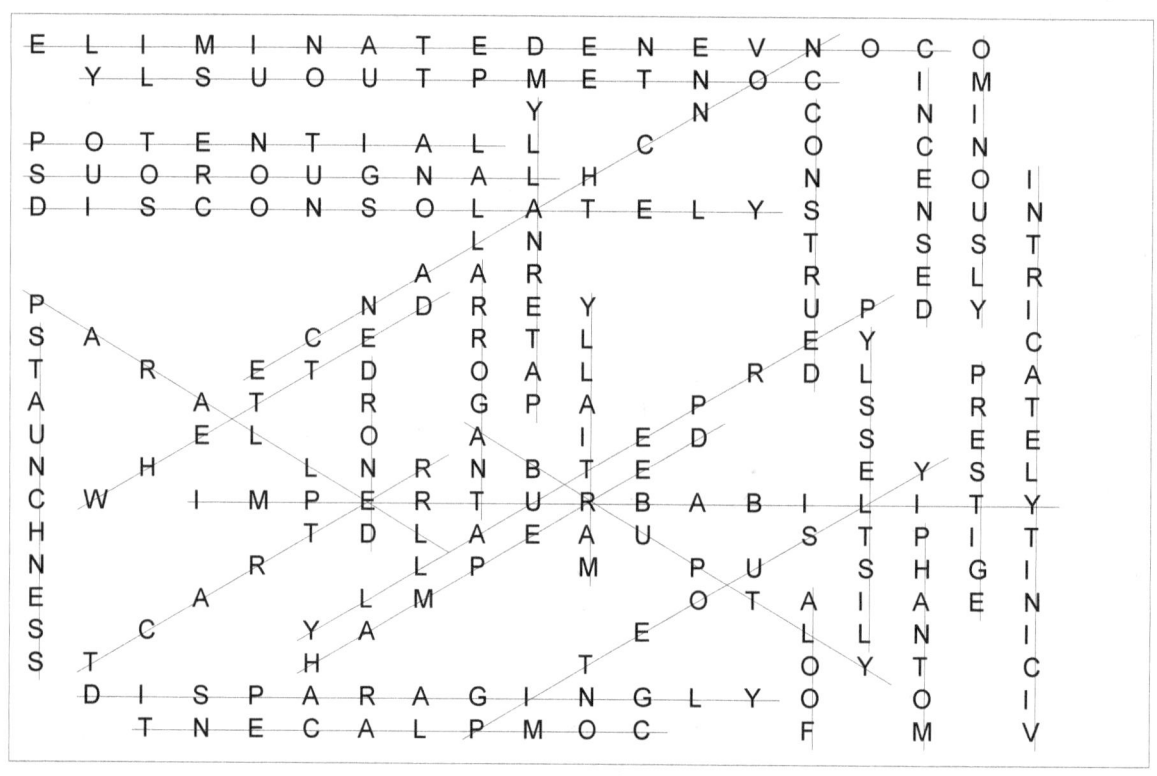

An image that appears only in the mind; ghost (7)
Assembled; came together (8)
Belittlingly; reducing in esteem (13)
Characteristic of not capable of being upset (16)
Continually (11)
Disdainfully; scornfully (14)
Distant; indifferent; apart (5)
Enraged; angered (8)
Equal distance apart at all points; a comparison indicating similarities (8)
Explained; interpreted (9)
Gotten rid of; left out of consideration (10)
Haughty; contemptuous; overbearing (8)
In a fatherly manner (10)
In a military or warlike manner (9)
Indifferently; unenthusiastically (10)
Latent; possible but not yet so (9)
Locality; proximity; neighborhood (8)

Made a low, dull, monotonous sound (6)
Moving to sympathy (9)
Prevented action or progress; impeded (8)
Renown; power to command admiration (8)
Self-satisfied; contented (10)
Sharpened (7)
Sorrowfully; dejectedly (14)
Steadfastness; resoluteness (11)
Still; sluggish; listless (10)
Suddenly (8)
Take back; withdraw (7)
Threateningly (9)
With a lack of concern; showing indifference (11)
With complexly arranged elements (11)

Red Pony Vocabulary Word Search 3

Words are placed backwards, forward, diagonally, up and down. Words listed below are included in the maze. Circle the hidden vocabulary words in the maze.

```
S T A U N C H N E S S D I C B A N C S N
L I S T L E S S L Y D I N O K R O O G H
B L G Y B S M N B R I S T N S R N N W G
J A V I C I N I T Y S P R T S O C S K B
T N E C A L P M O C C A I E E G H T R N
H G S Z V C Y T J N O R C M N A A R T Y
C U M O X L T Z J T N A A P S N L U E F
M O G L M P P W K K S G T L U T A E L V
Y R N P T I L D B S O I E A O D N D I D
L O X V E C N R N S L N L T I V C P M N
S U N W E R V O Z T A G Y I T G E A I S
U S Q I S N P N U L T L S V C F B T N M
O R J N M B E E C S E Y M E N R B E A H
E Q N C S N J D T Y L S U O U N E R T S
T L S E N V E E G U Y Y B P B R T N E J
I B G N W T T R L Y A Y T C M I M A D S
P R E S T I G E R Y Y L X L A M W L R C
G L J E V P L P M S Y M L R O B L E C
M V H D A L D M K S W F L Y P T C Y T J
J W V N A L D A T P H Y H F Q N D M R W
P Z Q R P T O H P O T E N T I A L J A N
G V A L L V O M W K V K H H H C K C P
J P B Y W Q C T F Q R C Y Y Q P H P T V
```

ABRUPTLY

ALOOF

ARROGANT

COMPLACENT

CONSTRUED

CONTEMPLATIVE

CONVENED

DISCONSOLATELY

DISPARAGINGLY

DRONED

ELIMINATED

HAMPERED

INCENSED

INTRICATELY

LANGUOROUS

LISTLESSLY

MARTIALLY

NONCHALANCE

OMINOUSLY

PARALLEL

PATERNALLY

PERPETUALLY

PHANTOM

PITEOUSLY

POTENTIAL

PRESTIGE

RAMBUNCTIOUSNESS

RETRACT

STAUNCHNESS

STRENUOUSLY

VICINITY

WHETTED

Red Pony Vocabulary Word Search 3 Answer Key

Words are placed backwards, forward, diagonally, up and down. Words listed below are included in the maze. Circle the hidden vocabulary words in the maze.

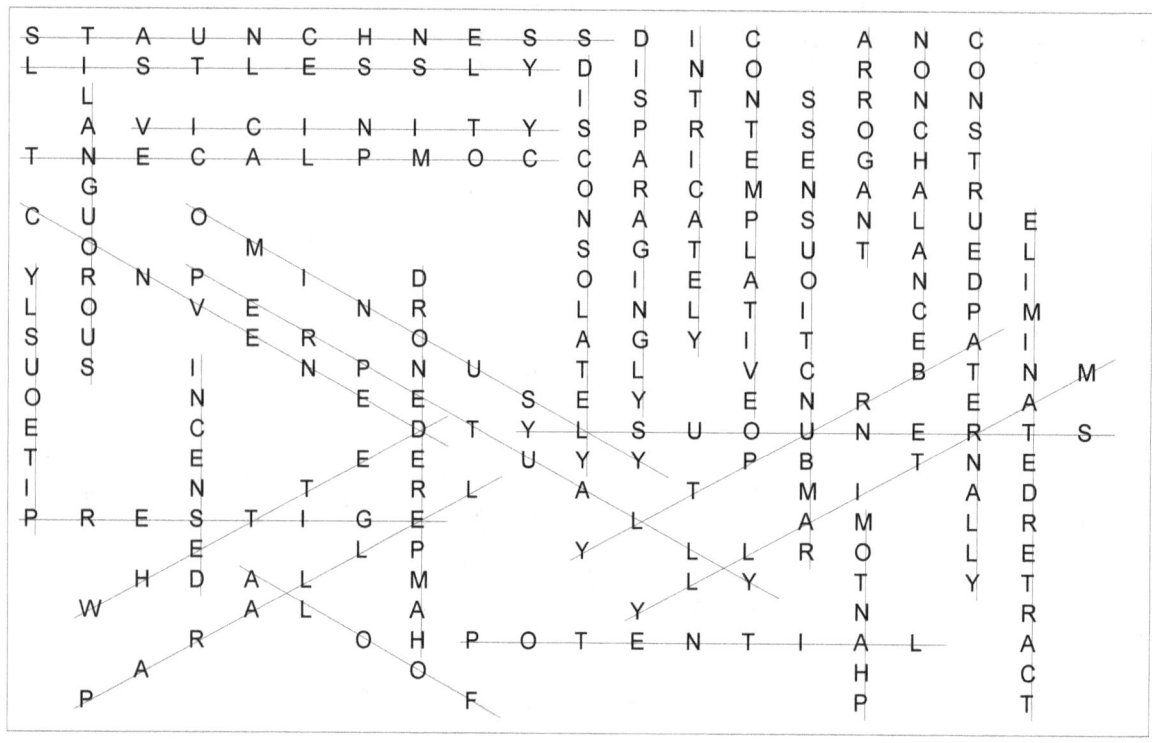

ABRUPTLY	HAMPERED	PHANTOM
ALOOF	INCENSED	PITEOUSLY
ARROGANT	INTRICATELY	POTENTIAL
COMPLACENT	LANGUOROUS	PRESTIGE
CONSTRUED	LISTLESSLY	RAMBUNCTIOUSNESS
CONTEMPLATIVE	MARTIALLY	RETRACT
CONVENED	NONCHALANCE	STAUNCHNESS
DISCONSOLATELY	OMINOUSLY	STRENUOUSLY
DISPARAGINGLY	PARALLEL	VICINITY
DRONED	PATERNALLY	WHETTED
ELIMINATED	PERPETUALLY	

Red Pony Vocabulary Word Search 4

Words are placed backwards, forward, diagonally, up and down. Words listed below are included in the maze. Circle the hidden vocabulary words in the maze.

```
L A N G U O R O U S A L O O F Q S D P G
W P N C R M V C S A R R O G A N T I E W
Y A F O D N L O T T Z H J N S F R S R R
D R O N E D G N A B R U P T L Y E P P V
E A P S R Y W V U P R L V S Z N N A E X
S L D T E T M E N R C Z B L Z L U R T S
N L Z R P I N N C G F D G J I P O A U Q
E E D U M L V E H R W X S S A G U G A G
C L N E A I I D N T M H T T X J S I L B
N D O D H B C H E K C L E F C W L N L W
I L N C P A I W S F E R Q S O H Y G Y G
K N C O R B N K S S N L Y H N E L L V Q
D X H M E R I T S A P L P Z T T Z Y N P
W V A P S U T L L C S P O B E T Y K D C
D H L L T T Y L S U O P T P M E T N O C
W N A A I R Y T O P X T E H P D D R L F
N G N C G E N N F Y P B N C L Y K E G F
J B C E E P I N S N H T T A Y D T L D
B R E N H M Y L E T A C I R T N I D V
T G C T O I J B Y R N M A F I G G A B Z
D I S C O N S O L A T E L Y V L Q C D J
E L I M I N A T E D O X X D E Y X T W Y
M A R T I A L L Y Z M P I T E O U S L Y
```

ABRUPTLY	ELIMINATED	PATERNALLY
ALOOF	HAMPERED	PERPETUALLY
ARROGANT	IMPERTURBABILITY	PHANTOM
COMPLACENT	INCENSED	PITEOUSLY
CONSTRUED	INTRICATELY	POTENTIAL
CONTEMPLATIVE	LANGUOROUS	PRESTIGE
CONTEMPTUOUSLY	LISTLESSLY	RETRACT
CONVENED	MARTIALLY	STAUNCHNESS
DISCONSOLATELY	NONCHALANCE	STRENUOUSLY
DISPARAGINGLY	OMINOUSLY	VICINITY
DRONED	PARALLEL	WHETTED

Red Pony Vocabulary Word Search 4 Answer Key

Words are placed backwards, forward, diagonally, up and down. Words listed below are included in the maze. Circle the hidden vocabulary words in the maze.

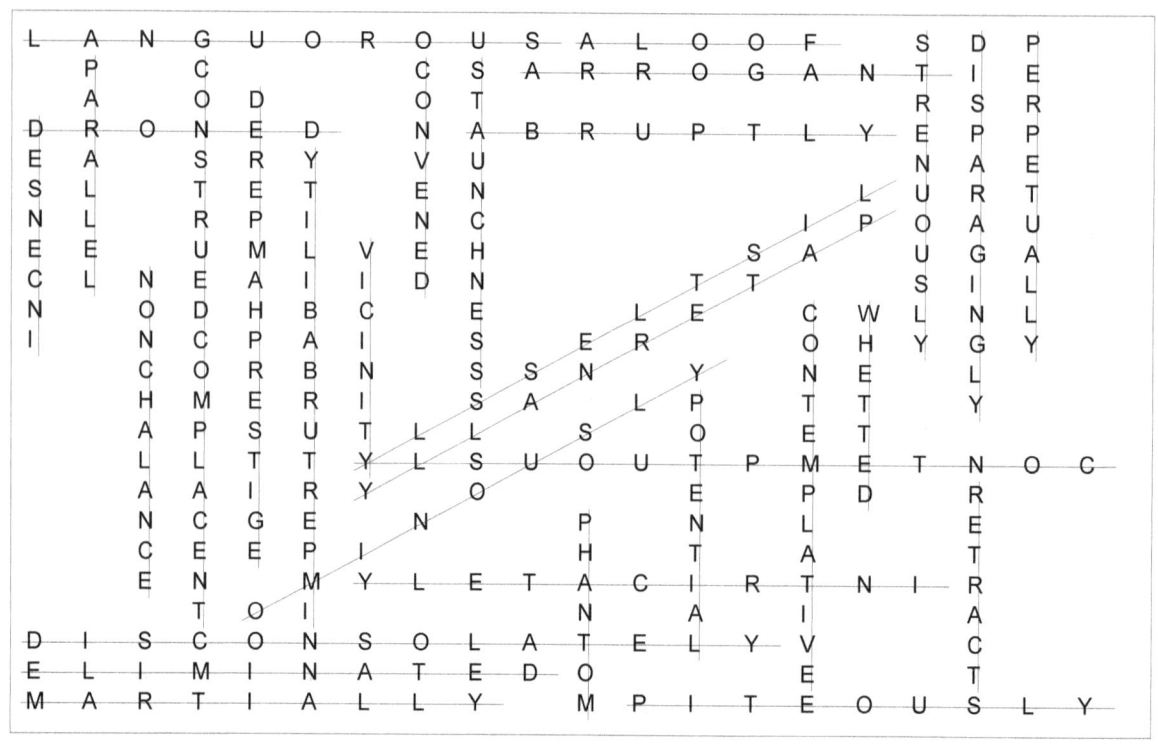

ABRUPTLY	ELIMINATED	PATERNALLY
ALOOF	HAMPERED	PERPETUALLY
ARROGANT	IMPERTURBABILITY	PHANTOM
COMPLACENT	INCENSED	PITEOUSLY
CONSTRUED	INTRICATELY	POTENTIAL
CONTEMPLATIVE	LANGUOROUS	PRESTIGE
CONTEMPTUOUSLY	LISTLESSLY	RETRACT
CONVENED	MARTIALLY	STAUNCHNESS
DISCONSOLATELY	NONCHALANCE	STRENUOUSLY
DISPARAGINGLY	OMINOUSLY	VICINITY
DRONED	PARALLEL	WHETTED

Red Pony Vocabulary Crossword 1

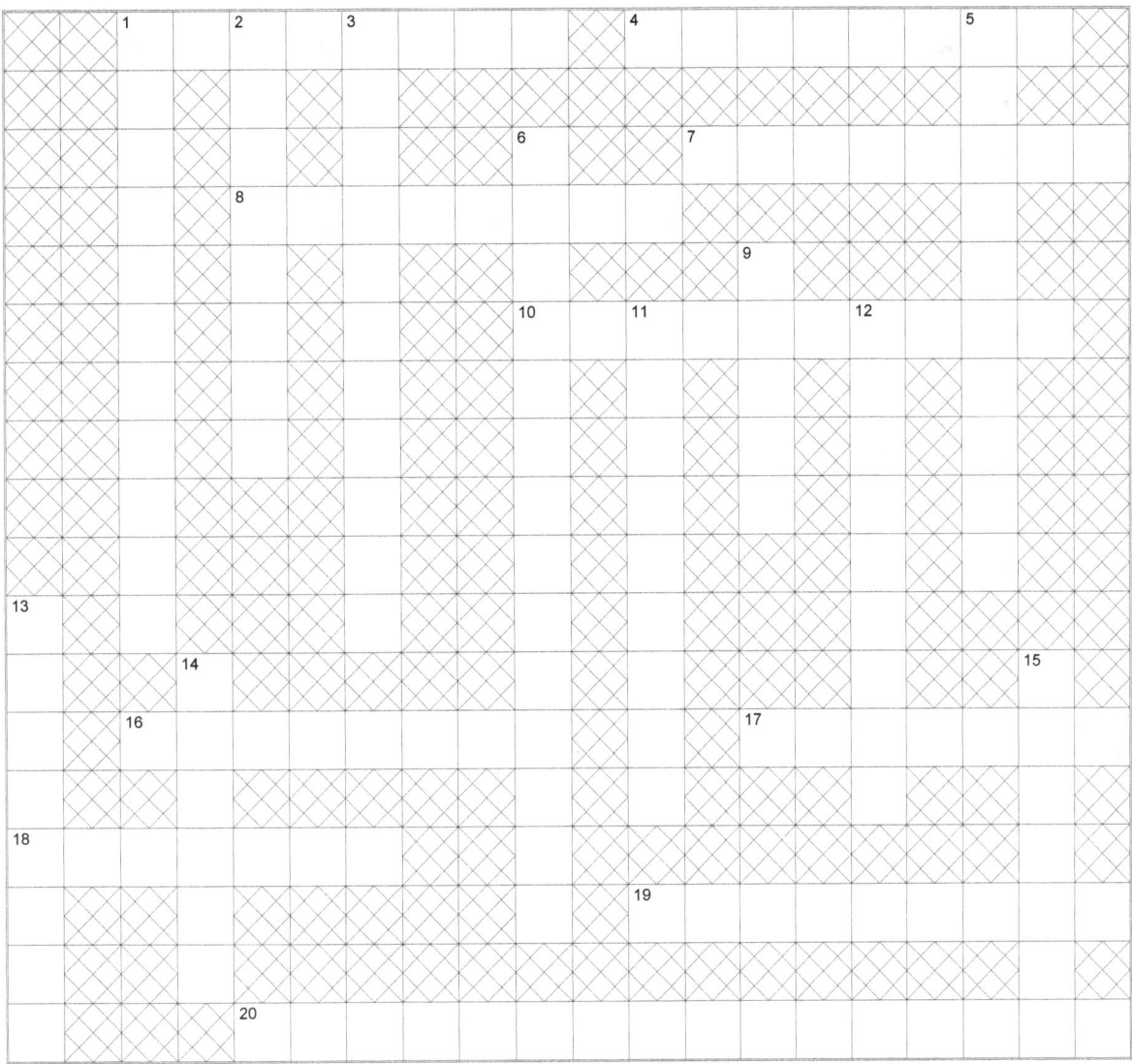

Across
1. Enraged; angered
4. Prevented action or progress; impeded
7. Renown; power to command admiration
8. Locality; proximity; neighborhood
10. Self-satisfied; contented
16. Haughty; contemptuous; overbearing
17. Sharpened
18. An image that appears only in the mind; ghost
19. Latent; possible but not yet so
20. Characteristic of not capable of being upset

Down
1. With complexly arranged elements
2. Assembled; came together
3. With a lack of concern; showing indifference
5. Gotten rid of; left out of consideration
6. Sorrowfully; dejectedly
9. Distant; indifferent; apart
11. In a military or warlike manner
12. Explained; interpreted
13. Suddenly
14. Made a low, dull, monotonous sound
15. Take back; withdraw

Red Pony Vocabulary Crossword 1 Answer Key

Across
1. Enraged; angered
4. Prevented action or progress; impeded
7. Renown; power to command admiration
8. Locality; proximity; neighborhood
10. Self-satisfied; contented
16. Haughty; contemptuous; overbearing
17. Sharpened
18. An image that appears only in the mind; ghost
19. Latent; possible but not yet so
20. Characteristic of not capable of being upset

Down
1. With complexly arranged elements
2. Assembled; came together
3. With a lack of concern; showing indifference
5. Gotten rid of; left out of consideration
6. Sorrowfully; dejectedly
9. Distant; indifferent; apart
11. In a military or warlike manner
12. Explained; interpreted
13. Suddenly
14. Made a low, dull, monotonous sound
15. Take back; withdraw

Red Pony Vocabulary Crossword 2

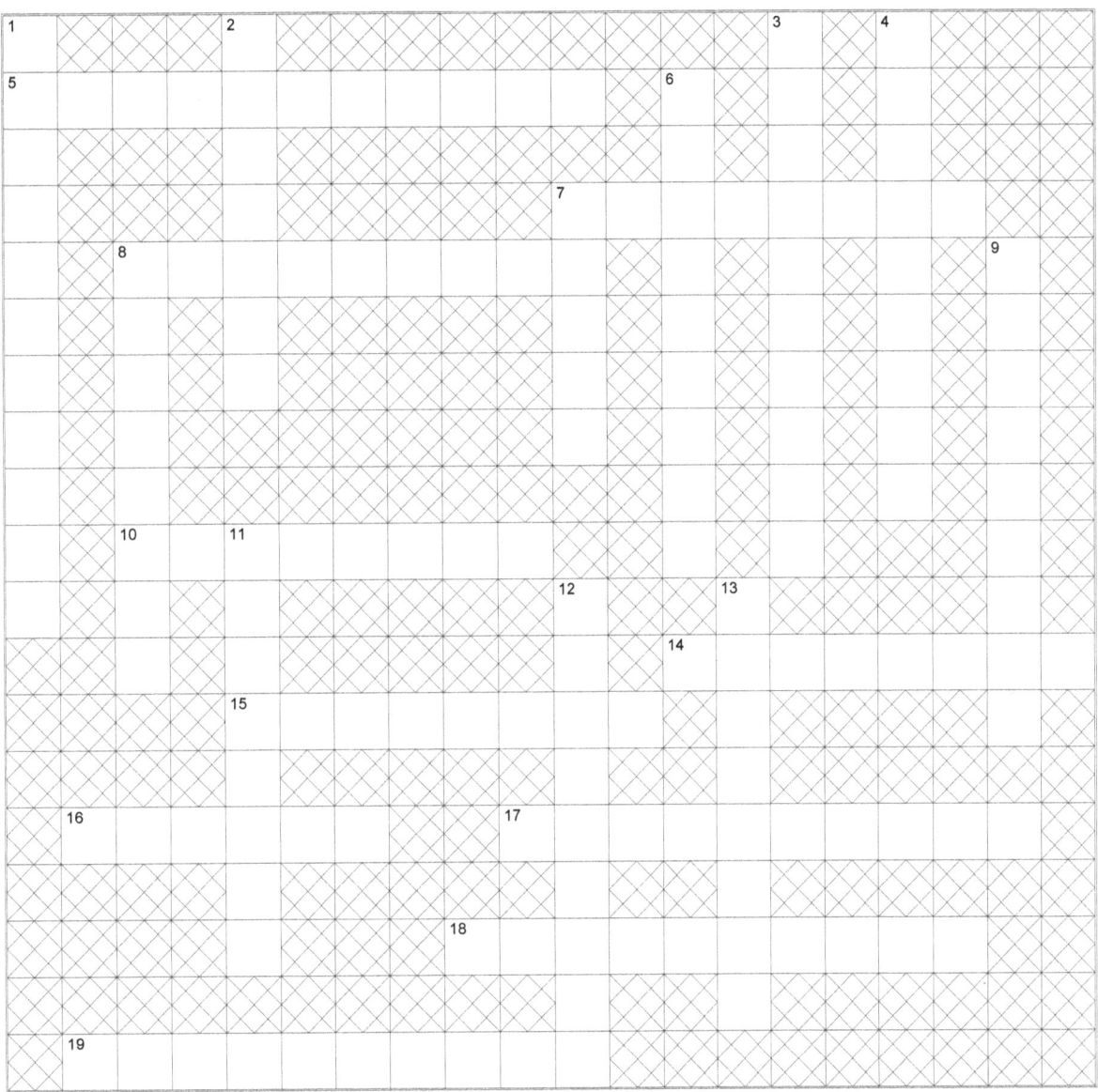

Across
5. With a lack of concern; showing indifference
7. Haughty; contemptuous; overbearing
8. Latent; possible but not yet so
10. Enraged; angered
14. Prevented action or progress; impeded
15. Locality; proximity; neighborhood
16. Made a low, dull, monotonous sound
17. Self-satisfied; contented
18. Indifferently; unenthusiastically
19. In a fatherly manner

Down
1. With complexly arranged elements
2. Sharpened
3. Still; sluggish; listless
4. Threateningly
6. In a military or warlike manner
7. Distant; indifferent; apart
8. Renown; power to command admiration
9. Explained; interpreted
11. Assembled; came together
12. Moving to sympathy
13. Equal distance apart at all points; a comparison indicating similarities

Red Pony Vocabulary Crossword 2 Answer Key

	1 I			2 W							3 L		4 O		
5	N	O	N	C	H	A	L	A	N	C	E	6 M	A	M	
	T			E								A		N	I
	R			T			7 A	R	R	O	G	A	N	T	
	I		8 P	O	T	E	N	T	I	A	L		U	O	9 C
	C		R	E			L		T		O		U	O
	A		E	D			O		I		R		S	N
	T		E				O		A		O		L	S
	E		S				F		L		U		Y	T
	L		T				L		Y		S			R
	10 I	N	11 C	E	N	S	E	D						
	Y		G	O						12 P		13 P			U
			E	N						I		14 H	A	M	P	E	R	E	D
				15 V	I	C	I	N	I	T	Y	R			D
				E						E		A			
		16 D	R	O	N	E	D		17 C	O	M	P	L	A	C	E	N	T
				E					U			L			
				D				18 L	I	S	T	L	E	S	S	L	Y
								L				L			
		19 P	A	T	E	R	N	A	L	L	Y				

Across
5. With a lack of concern; showing indifference
7. Haughty; contemptuous; overbearing
8. Latent; possible but not yet so
10. Enraged; angered
14. Prevented action or progress; impeded
15. Locality; proximity; neighborhood
16. Made a low, dull, monotonous sound
17. Self-satisfied; contented
18. Indifferently; unenthusiastically
19. In a fatherly manner

Down
1. With complexly arranged elements
2. Sharpened
3. Still; sluggish; listless
4. Threateningly
6. In a military or warlike manner
7. Distant; indifferent; apart
8. Renown; power to command admiration
9. Explained; interpreted
11. Assembled; came together
12. Moving to sympathy
13. Equal distance apart at all points; a comparison indicating similarities

Red Pony Vocabulary Crossword 3

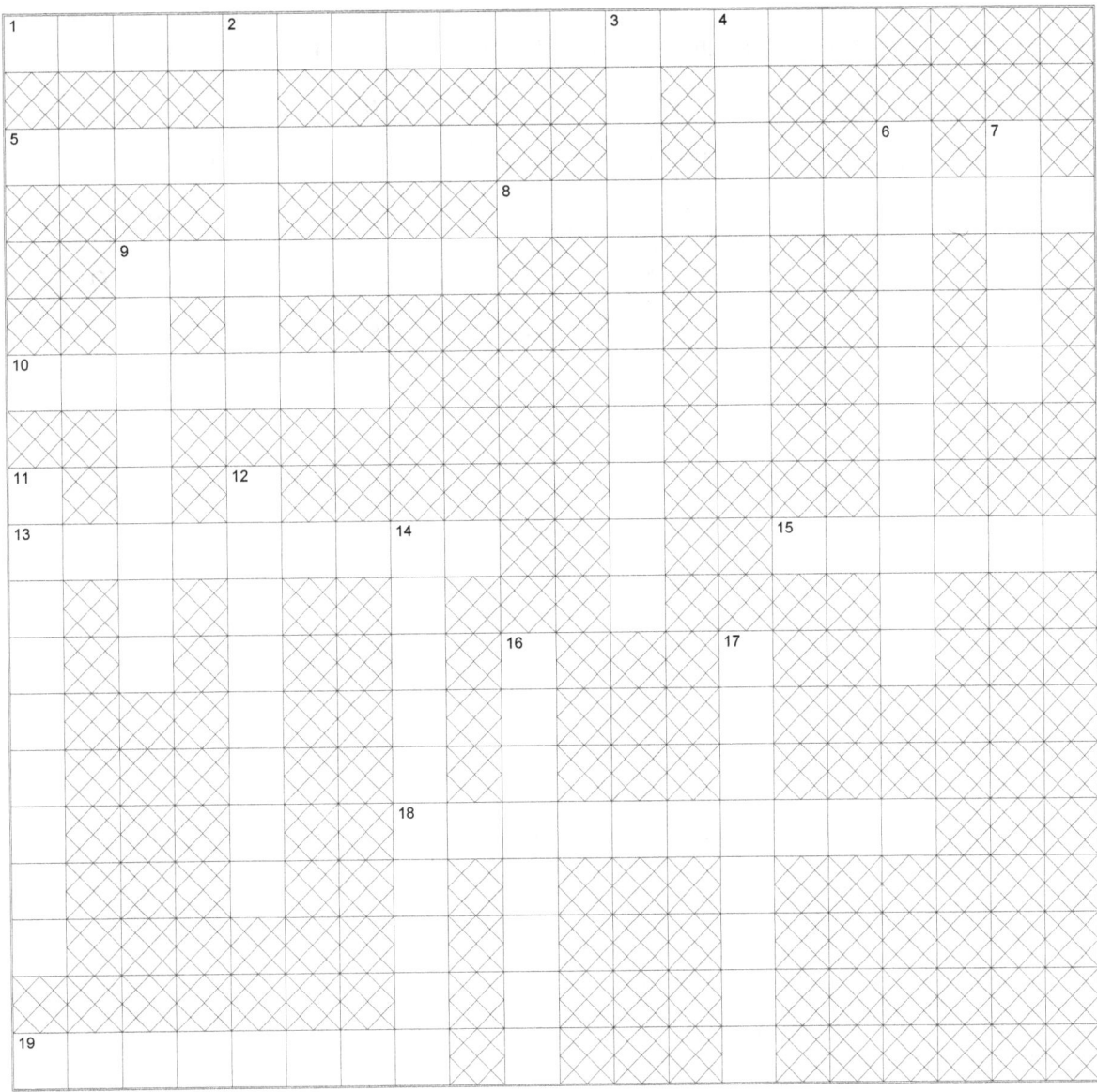

Across
1. Characteristic of not capable of being upset
5. Explained; interpreted
8. Continually
9. An image that appears only in the mind; ghost
10. Sharpened
13. Threateningly
15. Made a low, dull, monotonous sound
18. Gotten rid of; left out of consideration
19. Suddenly

Down
2. Take back; withdraw
3. With complexly arranged elements
4. Enraged; angered
6. Still; sluggish; listless
7. Distant; indifferent; apart
9. Renown; power to command admiration
11. Latent; possible but not yet so
12. Assembled; came together
14. Indifferently; unenthusiastically
16. Locality; proximity; neighborhood
17. Equal distance apart at all points; a comparison indicating similarities

Red Pony Vocabulary Crossword 3 Answer Key

Across
1. Characteristic of not capable of being upset
5. Explained; interpreted
8. Continually
9. An image that appears only in the mind; ghost
10. Sharpened
13. Threateningly
15. Made a low, dull, monotonous sound
18. Gotten rid of; left out of consideration
19. Suddenly

Down
2. Take back; withdraw
3. With complexly arranged elements
4. Enraged; angered
6. Still; sluggish; listless
7. Distant; indifferent; apart
9. Renown; power to command admiration
11. Latent; possible but not yet so
12. Assembled; came together
14. Indifferently; unenthusiastically
16. Locality; proximity; neighborhood
17. Equal distance apart at all points; a comparison indicating similarities

Red Pony Vocabulary Crossword 4

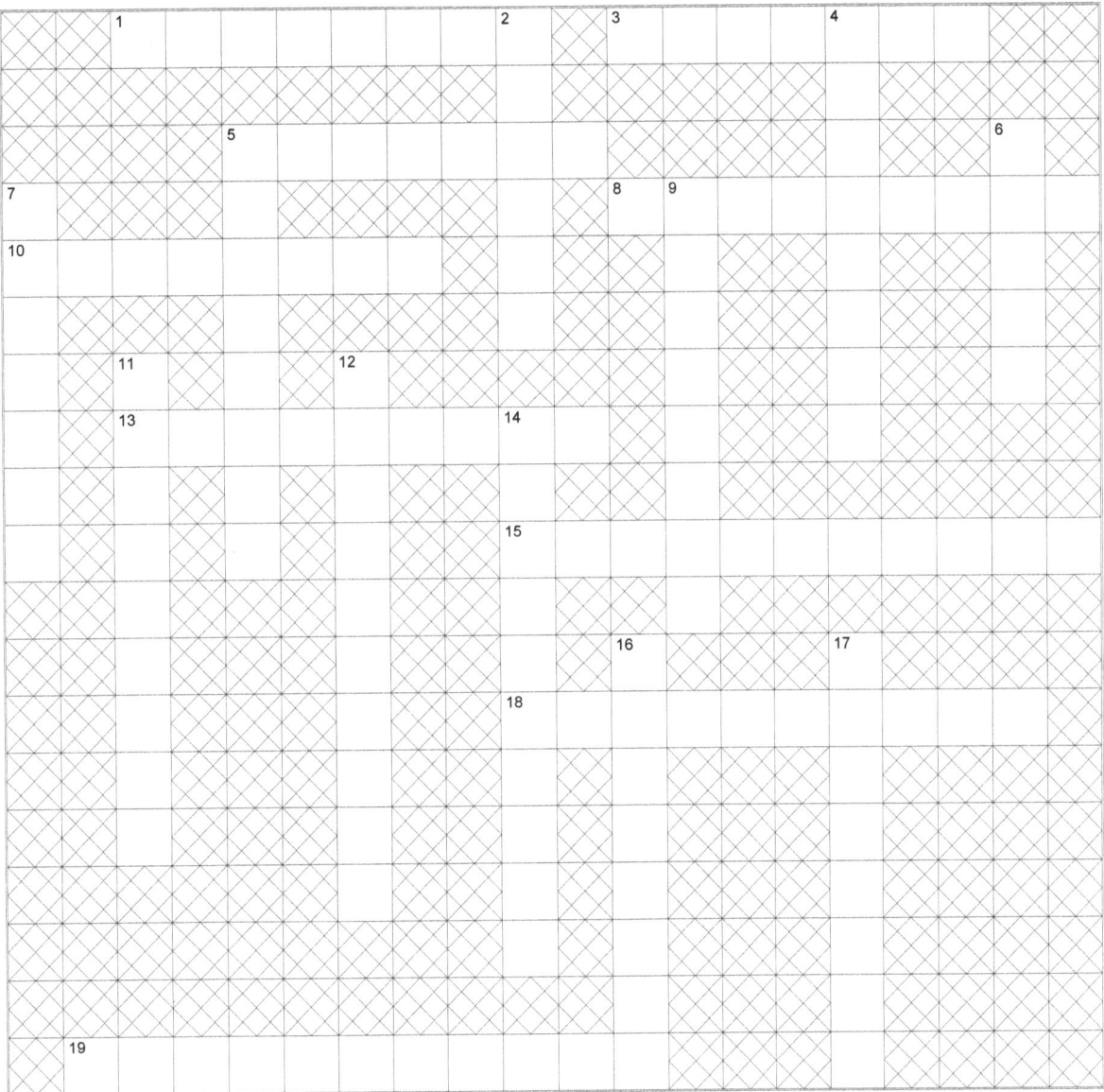

Across
1. Assembled; came together
3. Take back; withdraw
5. An image that appears only in the mind; ghost
8. Moving to sympathy
10. Prevented action or progress; impeded
13. Threateningly
15. Energetically; vigorously; actively
18. Gotten rid of; left out of consideration
19. With complexly arranged elements

Down
2. Made a low, dull, monotonous sound
4. Haughty; contemptuous; overbearing
5. Renown; power to command admiration
6. Distant; indifferent; apart
7. Sharpened
9. Enraged; angered
11. Latent; possible but not yet so
12. Self-satisfied; contented
14. Indifferently; unenthusiastically
16. Locality; proximity; neighborhood
17. Equal distance apart at all points; a comparison indicating similarities

Red Pony Vocabulary Crossword 4 Answer Key

Across
1. Assembled; came together
3. Take back; withdraw
5. An image that appears only in the mind; ghost
8. Moving to sympathy
10. Prevented action or progress; impeded
13. Threateningly
15. Energetically; vigorously; actively
18. Gotten rid of; left out of consideration
19. With complexly arranged elements

Down
2. Made a low, dull, monotonous sound
4. Haughty; contemptuous; overbearing
5. Renown; power to command admiration
6. Distant; indifferent; apart
7. Sharpened
9. Enraged; angered
11. Latent; possible but not yet so
12. Self-satisfied; contented
14. Indifferently; unenthusiastically
16. Locality; proximity; neighborhood
17. Equal distance apart at all points; a comparison indicating similarities

Red Pony Vocabulary Juggle Letters 1

1. CTAERTR = 1. _____
   Take back; withdraw

2. AOSUNGULOR = 2. _____
   Still; sluggish; listless

3. TEYANCIRTLI = 3. _____
   With complexly arranged elements

4. ODNEVNEC = 4. _____
   Assembled; came together

5. TYLSAOSNOLCIDE = 5. _____
   Sorrowfully; dejectedly

6. ENTNSUSHCAS = 6. _____
   Steadfastness; resoluteness

7. IALETPNOT = 7. _____
   Latent; possible but not yet so

8. BEIIRTMALUIPBYTR = 8. _____
   Characteristic of not capable of being upset

9. TSLLLSYESI = 9. _____
   Indifferently; unenthusiastically

10. DDOERN = 10. _____
    Made a low, dull, monotonous sound

11. ERLPUETAYLP = 11. _____
    Continually

12. LLAPERAL = 12. _____
    Equal distance apart at all points; a comparison indicating similarities

13. OTMPAHN = 13. _____
    An image that appears only in the mind; ghost

14. TUCMOENTUSYLPO = 14. _____
    Disdainfully; scornfully

15. TSELSRNOYUU = 15. _____
    Energetically; vigorously; actively

Red Pony Vocabulary Juggle Letters 1 Answer Key

1. CTAERTR = 1. RETRACT
   Take back; withdraw

2. AOSUNGULOR = 2. LANGUOROUS
   Still; sluggish; listless

3. TEYANCIRTLI = 3. INTRICATELY
   With complexly arranged elements

4. ODNEVNEC = 4. CONVENED
   Assembled; came together

5. TYLSAOSNOLCIDE = 5. DISCONSOLATELY
   Sorrowfully; dejectedly

6. ENTNSUSHCAS = 6. STAUNCHNESS
   Steadfastness; resoluteness

7. IALETPNOT = 7. POTENTIAL
   Latent; possible but not yet so

8. BEIIRTMALUIPBYTR = 8. IMPERTURBABILITY
   Characteristic of not capable of being upset

9. TSLLLSYESI = 9. LISTLESSLY
   Indifferently; unenthusiastically

10. DDOERN = 10. DRONED
    Made a low, dull, monotonous sound

11. ERLPUETAYLP = 11. PERPETUALLY
    Continually

12. LLAPERAL = 12. PARALLEL
    Equal distance apart at all points; a comparison indicating similarities

13. OTMPAHN = 13. PHANTOM
    An image that appears only in the mind; ghost

14. TUCMOENTUSYLPO = 14. CONTEMPTUOUSLY
    Disdainfully; scornfully

15. TSELSRNOYUU = 15. STRENUOUSLY
    Energetically; vigorously; actively

Red Pony Vocabulary Juggle Letters 2

1. LTLSLISESY = 1. _____
   Indifferently; unenthusiastically

2. BLPARTYU = 2. _____
   Suddenly

3. MIOSNYOLU = 3. _____
   Threateningly

4. FAOOL = 4. _____
   Distant; indifferent; apart

5. OEDDNR = 5. _____
   Made a low, dull, monotonous sound

6. TSYLMTCEPUNOUO = 6. _____
   Disdainfully; scornfully

7. EPEHMRDA = 7. _____
   Prevented action or progress; impeded

8. LAOCNCNEANH = 8. _____
   With a lack of concern; showing indifference

9. PAOCCTMLNE = 9. _____
   Self-satisfied; contented

10. AITTELONP =10. _____
    Latent; possible but not yet so

11. PLULTYERAEP =11. _____
    Continually

12. NURSETDCO =12. _____
    Explained; interpreted

13. ANPTLYEALR =13. _____
    In a fatherly manner

14. DNVEOECN =14. _____
    Assembled; came together

15. LPAELRAL =15. _____
    Equal distance apart at all points; a comparison indicating similarities

Red Pony Vocabulary Juggle Letters 2 Answer Key

1. LTLSLISESY = 1. LISTLESSLY
Indifferently; unenthusiastically

2. BLPARTYU = 2. ABRUPTLY
Suddenly

3. MIOSNYOLU = 3. OMINOUSLY
Threateningly

4. FAOOL = 4. ALOOF
Distant; indifferent; apart

5. OEDDNR = 5. DRONED
Made a low, dull, monotonous sound

6. TSYLMTCEPUNOUO = 6. CONTEMPTUOUSLY
Disdainfully; scornfully

7. EPEHMRDA = 7. HAMPERED
Prevented action or progress; impeded

8. LAOCNCNEANH = 8. NONCHALANCE
With a lack of concern; showing indifference

9. PAOCCTMLNE = 9. COMPLACENT
Self-satisfied; contented

10. AITTELONP = 10. POTENTIAL
Latent; possible but not yet so

11. PLULTYERAEP = 11. PERPETUALLY
Continually

12. NURSETDCO = 12. CONSTRUED
Explained; interpreted

13. ANPTLYEALR = 13. PATERNALLY
In a fatherly manner

14. DNVEOECN = 14. CONVENED
Assembled; came together

15. LPAELRAL = 15. PARALLEL
Equal distance apart at all points; a comparison indicating similarities

Red Pony Vocabulary Juggle Letters 3

1. DNESTORCU = 1. _____
   Explained; interpreted

2. NVIITICY = 2. _____
   Locality; proximity; neighborhood

3. TLRABUPY = 3. _____
   Suddenly

4. EAMREDHP = 4. _____
   Prevented action or progress; impeded

5. SONAROUUGL = 5. _____
   Still; sluggish; listless

6. YSULIPEOT = 6. _____
   Moving to sympathy

7. EINDCSNE = 7. _____
   Enraged; angered

8. TPONILTEA = 8. _____
   Latent; possible but not yet so

9. GPNYADSAIGILR = 9. _____
   Belittlingly; reducing in esteem

10. NEUTOCUYTOMSPL =10. _____
    Disdainfully; scornfully

11. EMETAILTCNPVO =11. _____
    Thoughtful; meditative

12. EEWTHTD =12. _____
    Sharpened

13. LCNCOTAEMP =13. _____
    Self-satisfied; contented

14. SERUSSBNNCOIUMTA =14. _____
    Boisterousness; rowdiness

15. RNGROAAT =15. _____
    Haughty; contemptuous; overbearing

Red Pony Vocabulary Juggle Letters 3 Answer Key

1. DNESTORCU = 1. CONSTRUED
   Explained; interpreted

2. NVIITICY = 2. VICINITY
   Locality; proximity; neighborhood

3. TLRABUPY = 3. ABRUPTLY
   Suddenly

4. EAMREDHP = 4. HAMPERED
   Prevented action or progress; impeded

5. SONAROUUGL = 5. LANGUOROUS
   Still; sluggish; listless

6. YSULIPEOT = 6. PITEOUSLY
   Moving to sympathy

7. EINDCSNE = 7. INCENSED
   Enraged; angered

8. TPONILTEA = 8. POTENTIAL
   Latent; possible but not yet so

9. GPNYADSAIGILR = 9. DISPARAGINGLY
   Belittlingly; reducing in esteem

10. NEUTOCUYTOMSPL = 10. CONTEMPTUOUSLY
    Disdainfully; scornfully

11. EMETAILTCNPVO = 11. CONTEMPLATIVE
    Thoughtful; meditative

12. EEWTHTD = 12. WHETTED
    Sharpened

13. LCNCOTAEMP = 13. COMPLACENT
    Self-satisfied; contented

14. SERUSSBNNCOIUMTA = 14. RAMBUNCTIOUSNESS
    Boisterousness; rowdiness

15. RNGROAAT = 15. ARROGANT
    Haughty; contemptuous; overbearing

Red Pony Vocabulary Juggle Letters 4

1. NIECSDEN = 1. _____
   Enraged; angered

2. HPTMNOA = 2. _____
   An image that appears only in the mind; ghost

3. ANTOMVELPEICT = 3. _____
   Thoughtful; meditative

4. TALNPIOTE = 4. _____
   Latent; possible but not yet so

5. DCTNEOSUR = 5. _____
   Explained; interpreted

6. YPOSEUILT = 6. _____
   Moving to sympathy

7. ESUASTSHCNN = 7. _____
   Steadfastness; resoluteness

8. LAMTLYIAR = 8. _____
   In a military or warlike manner

9. ARLYLNTEAP = 9. _____
   In a fatherly manner

10. CRTETRA =10. _____
    Take back; withdraw

11. NGTARROA =11. _____
    Haughty; contemptuous; overbearing

12. ENVNCEDO =12. _____
    Assembled; came together

13. ALLEPLAR =13. _____
    Equal distance apart at all points; a comparison indicating similarities

14. OFOLA =14. _____
    Distant; indifferent; apart

15. IAETLENIMD =15. _____
    Gotten rid of; left out of consideration

Red Pony Vocabulary Juggle Letters 4 Answer Key

1. NIECSDEN = 1. INCENSED
   Enraged; angered

2. HPTMNOA = 2. PHANTOM
   An image that appears only in the mind; ghost

3. ANTOMVELPEICT = 3. CONTEMPLATIVE
   Thoughtful; meditative

4. TALNPIOTE = 4. POTENTIAL
   Latent; possible but not yet so

5. DCTNEOSUR = 5. CONSTRUED
   Explained; interpreted

6. YPOSEUILT = 6. PITEOUSLY
   Moving to sympathy

7. ESUASTSHCNN = 7. STAUNCHNESS
   Steadfastness; resoluteness

8. LAMTLYIAR = 8. MARTIALLY
   In a military or warlike manner

9. ARLYLNTEAP = 9. PATERNALLY
   In a fatherly manner

10. CRTETRA =10. RETRACT
    Take back; withdraw

11. NGTARROA =11. ARROGANT
    Haughty; contemptuous; overbearing

12. ENVNCEDO =12. CONVENED
    Assembled; came together

13. ALLEPLAR =13. PARALLEL
    Equal distance apart at all points; a comparison indicating similarities

14. OFOLA =14. ALOOF
    Distant; indifferent; apart

15. IAETLENIMD =15. ELIMINATED
    Gotten rid of; left out of consideration

ABRUPTLY	Suddenly
ALOOF	Distant; indifferent; apart
ARROGANT	Haughty; contemptuous; overbearing
COMPLACENT	Self-satisfied; contented
CONSTRUED	Explained; interpreted
CONTEMPLATIVE	Thoughtful; meditative

CONTEMPTUOUSLY	Disdainfully; scornfully
CONVENED	Assembled; came together
DISCONSOLATELY	Sorrowfully; dejectedly
DISPARAGINGLY	Belittlingly; reducing in esteem
DRONED	Made a low, dull, monotonous sound
ELIMINATED	Gotten rid of; left out of consideration

HAMPERED	Prevented action or progress; impeded
IMPERTURBABILITY	Characteristic of not capable of being upset
INCENSED	Enraged; angered
INTRICATELY	With complexly arranged elements
LANGUOROUS	Still; sluggish; listless
LISTLESSLY	Indifferently; unenthusiastically

MARTIALLY	In a military or warlike manner
NONCHALANCE	With a lack of concern; showing indifference
OMINOUSLY	Threateningly
PARALLEL	Equal distance apart at all points; a comparison indicating similarities
PATERNALLY	In a fatherly manner
PERPETUALLY	Continually

PHANTOM	An image that appears only in the mind; ghost
PITEOUSLY	Moving to sympathy
POTENTIAL	Latent; possible but not yet so
PRESTIGE	Renown; power to command admiration
RAMBUNCTIOUSNESS	Boisterousness; rowdiness
RETRACT	Take back; withdraw

STAUNCHNESS	Steadfastness; resoluteness
STRENUOUSLY	Energetically; vigorously; actively
VICINITY	Locality; proximity; neighborhood
WHETTED	Sharpened

Red Pony Vocabulary

STRENUOUSLY	CONSTRUED	HAMPERED	MARTIALLY	INCENSED
DISCONSOLATELY	PATERNALLY	DRONED	RETRACT	IMPERTURBABILITY
PITEOUSLY	PRESTIGE	FREE SPACE	INTRICATELY	POTENTIAL
PHANTOM	ABRUPTLY	PERPETUALLY	VICINITY	PARALLEL
STAUNCHNESS	LISTLESSLY	LANGUOROUS	DISPARAGINGLY	CONVENED

Red Pony Vocabulary

NONCHALANCE	CONTEMPLATIVE	ELIMINATED	ARROGANT	ALOOF
CONTEMPTUOUSLY	OMINOUSLY	RAMBUNCTIOUSNESS	WHETTED	CONVENED
DISPARAGINGLY	LANGUOROUS	FREE SPACE	STAUNCHNESS	PARALLEL
VICINITY	PERPETUALLY	ABRUPTLY	PHANTOM	POTENTIAL
INTRICATELY	COMPLACENT	PRESTIGE	PITEOUSLY	IMPERTURBABILITY

Red Pony Vocabulary

PERPETUALLY	VICINITY	LANGUOROUS	MARTIALLY	ABRUPTLY
ELIMINATED	LISTLESSLY	COMPLACENT	WHETTED	HAMPERED
INCENSED	INTRICATELY	FREE SPACE	DISCONSOLATELY	OMINOUSLY
PATERNALLY	DISPARAGINGLY	CONVENED	PARALLEL	CONSTRUED
PRESTIGE	RAMBUNCTIOUSNESS	DRONED	ARROGANT	NONCHALANCE

Red Pony Vocabulary

PITEOUSLY	STRENUOUSLY	STAUNCHNESS	RETRACT	POTENTIAL
IMPERTURBABILITY	PHANTOM	ALOOF	CONTEMPLATIVE	NONCHALANCE
ARROGANT	DRONED	FREE SPACE	PRESTIGE	CONSTRUED
PARALLEL	CONVENED	DISPARAGINGLY	PATERNALLY	OMINOUSLY
DISCONSOLATELY	CONTEMPTUOUSLY	INTRICATELY	INCENSED	HAMPERED

Red Pony Vocabulary

PARALLEL	DISCONSOLATELY	ELIMINATED	ABRUPTLY	STRENUOUSLY
OMINOUSLY	PRESTIGE	INTRICATELY	CONTEMPTUOUSLY	PERPETUALLY
NONCHALANCE	LANGUOROUS	FREE SPACE	IMPERTURBABILITY	STAUNCHNESS
RETRACT	HAMPERED	ALOOF	PHANTOM	WHETTED
DISPARAGINGLY	COMPLACENT	VICINITY	INCENSED	PITEOUSLY

Red Pony Vocabulary

DRONED	CONSTRUED	CONVENED	ARROGANT	LISTLESSLY
CONTEMPLATIVE	POTENTIAL	PATERNALLY	MARTIALLY	PITEOUSLY
INCENSED	VICINITY	FREE SPACE	DISPARAGINGLY	WHETTED
PHANTOM	ALOOF	HAMPERED	RETRACT	STAUNCHNESS
IMPERTURBABILITY	RAMBUNCTIOUSNESS	LANGUOROUS	NONCHALANCE	PERPETUALLY

Red Pony Vocabulary

VICINITY	CONVENED	WHETTED	DRONED	PRESTIGE
COMPLACENT	DISPARAGINGLY	CONTEMPLATIVE	ABRUPTLY	DISCONSOLATELY
MARTIALLY	ARROGANT	FREE SPACE	RETRACT	CONTEMPTUOUSLY
OMINOUSLY	LISTLESSLY	LANGUOROUS	HAMPERED	NONCHALANCE
IMPERTURBABILITY	POTENTIAL	INCENSED	ALOOF	INTRICATELY

Red Pony Vocabulary

PATERNALLY	CONSTRUED	STAUNCHNESS	PARALLEL	ELIMINATED
PERPETUALLY	PHANTOM	PITEOUSLY	RAMBUNCTIOUSNESS	INTRICATELY
ALOOF	INCENSED	FREE SPACE	IMPERTURBABILITY	NONCHALANCE
HAMPERED	LANGUOROUS	LISTLESSLY	OMINOUSLY	CONTEMPTUOUSLY
RETRACT	STRENUOUSLY	ARROGANT	MARTIALLY	DISCONSOLATELY

Red Pony Vocabulary

ALOOF	INCENSED	NONCHALANCE	STAUNCHNESS	PATERNALLY
RETRACT	STRENUOUSLY	LANGUOROUS	ARROGANT	PRESTIGE
PERPETUALLY	POTENTIAL	FREE SPACE	VICINITY	DISCONSOLATELY
HAMPERED	PHANTOM	ABRUPTLY	CONTEMPTUOUSLY	CONSTRUED
DISPARAGINGLY	MARTIALLY	CONTEMPLATIVE	COMPLACENT	INTRICATELY

INS

Red Pony Vocabulary

DRONED	CONVENED	LISTLESSLY	IMPERTURBABILITY	ELIMINATED
WHETTED	RAMBUNCTIOUSNESS	PITEOUSLY	OMINOUSLY	INTRICATELY
COMPLACENT	CONTEMPLATIVE	FREE SPACE	DISPARAGINGLY	CONSTRUED
CONTEMPTUOUSLY	ABRUPTLY	PHANTOM	HAMPERED	DISCONSOLATELY
VICINITY	PARALLEL	POTENTIAL	PERPETUALLY	PRESTIGE

Red Pony Vocabulary

DISPARAGINGLY	ELIMINATED	HAMPERED	ABRUPTLY	LANGUOROUS
ALOOF	CONSTRUED	PHANTOM	LISTLESSLY	DISCONSOLATELY
POTENTIAL	PERPETUALLY	FREE SPACE	COMPLACENT	PITEOUSLY
PRESTIGE	OMINOUSLY	VICINITY	RETRACT	INTRICATELY
MARTIALLY	IMPERTURBABILITY	RAMBUNCTIOUSNESS	ARROGANT	INCENSED

Red Pony Vocabulary

WHETTED	DRONED	CONVENED	PARALLEL	CONTEMPTUOUSLY
STAUNCHNESS	STRENUOUSLY	CONTEMPLATIVE	PATERNALLY	INCENSED
ARROGANT	RAMBUNCTIOUSNESS	FREE SPACE	MARTIALLY	INTRICATELY
RETRACT	VICINITY	OMINOUSLY	PRESTIGE	PITEOUSLY
COMPLACENT	NONCHALANCE	PERPETUALLY	POTENTIAL	DISCONSOLATELY

Red Pony Vocabulary

CONTEMPTUOUSLY	ABRUPTLY	PHANTOM	LISTLESSLY	DRONED
CONVENED	DISPARAGINGLY	RETRACT	COMPLACENT	CONSTRUED
ALOOF	LANGUOROUS	FREE SPACE	PITEOUSLY	ELIMINATED
PERPETUALLY	POTENTIAL	OMINOUSLY	RAMBUNCTIOUSNESS	WHETTED
PARALLEL	DISCONSOLATELY	STRENUOUSLY	PATERNALLY	NONCHALANCE

Red Pony Vocabulary

CONTEMPLATIVE	INTRICATELY	ARROGANT	HAMPERED	IMPERTURBABILITY
INCENSED	PRESTIGE	STAUNCHNESS	VICINITY	NONCHALANCE
PATERNALLY	STRENUOUSLY	FREE SPACE	PARALLEL	WHETTED
RAMBUNCTIOUSNESS	OMINOUSLY	POTENTIAL	PERPETUALLY	ELIMINATED
PITEOUSLY	MARTIALLY	LANGUOROUS	ALOOF	CONSTRUED

Red Pony Vocabulary

PITEOUSLY	ARROGANT	PHANTOM	CONTEMPTUOUSLY	LISTLESSLY
CONVENED	STRENUOUSLY	DISCONSOLATELY	RETRACT	VICINITY
INCENSED	HAMPERED	FREE SPACE	DISPARAGINGLY	ELIMINATED
PARALLEL	LANGUOROUS	POTENTIAL	IMPERTURBABILITY	PRESTIGE
DRONED	COMPLACENT	OMINOUSLY	WHETTED	CONTEMPLATIVE

Red Pony Vocabulary

PERPETUALLY	PATERNALLY	RAMBUNCTIOUSNESS	ALOOF	STAUNCHNESS
MARTIALLY	NONCHALANCE	INTRICATELY	CONSTRUED	CONTEMPLATIVE
WHETTED	OMINOUSLY	FREE SPACE	DRONED	PRESTIGE
IMPERTURBABILITY	POTENTIAL	LANGUOROUS	PARALLEL	ELIMINATED
DISPARAGINGLY	ABRUPTLY	HAMPERED	INCENSED	VICINITY

Red Pony Vocabulary

PARALLEL	STAUNCHNESS	RAMBUNCTIOUSNESS	CONTEMPLATIVE	INTRICATELY
PITEOUSLY	INCENSED	DISPARAGINGLY	COMPLACENT	ELIMINATED
PHANTOM	ABRUPTLY	FREE SPACE	VICINITY	HAMPERED
PERPETUALLY	LANGUOROUS	ALOOF	OMINOUSLY	IMPERTURBABILITY
LISTLESSLY	PATERNALLY	STRENUOUSLY	DRONED	MARTIALLY

Red Pony Vocabulary

DISCONSOLATELY	CONTEMPTUOUSLY	NONCHALANCE	WHETTED	RETRACT
PRESTIGE	CONSTRUED	CONVENED	POTENTIAL	MARTIALLY
DRONED	STRENUOUSLY	FREE SPACE	LISTLESSLY	IMPERTURBABILITY
OMINOUSLY	ALOOF	LANGUOROUS	PERPETUALLY	HAMPERED
VICINITY	ARROGANT	ABRUPTLY	PHANTOM	ELIMINATED

Red Pony Vocabulary

PATERNALLY	INTRICATELY	LANGUOROUS	ARROGANT	DISPARAGINGLY
LISTLESSLY	ABRUPTLY	CONTEMPLATIVE	ELIMINATED	POTENTIAL
DISCONSOLATELY	PHANTOM	FREE SPACE	ALOOF	COMPLACENT
CONSTRUED	STRENUOUSLY	DRONED	NONCHALANCE	RAMBUNCTIOUSNESS
OMINOUSLY	CONVENED	CONTEMPTUOUSLY	PITEOUSLY	IMPERTURBABILITY

Red Pony Vocabulary

PERPETUALLY	MARTIALLY	WHETTED	PRESTIGE	STAUNCHNESS
HAMPERED	RETRACT	VICINITY	INCENSED	IMPERTURBABILITY
PITEOUSLY	CONTEMPTUOUSLY	FREE SPACE	OMINOUSLY	RAMBUNCTIOUSNESS
NONCHALANCE	DRONED	STRENUOUSLY	CONSTRUED	COMPLACENT
ALOOF	PARALLEL	PHANTOM	DISCONSOLATELY	POTENTIAL

Red Pony Vocabulary

POTENTIAL	DISPARAGINGLY	CONTEMPTUOUSLY	PRESTIGE	PERPETUALLY
RAMBUNCTIOUSNESS	RETRACT	COMPLACENT	VICINITY	NONCHALANCE
MARTIALLY	LANGUOROUS	FREE SPACE	PHANTOM	CONTEMPLATIVE
IMPERTURBABILITY	INTRICATELY	INCENSED	DISCONSOLATELY	STAUNCHNESS
CONSTRUED	LISTLESSLY	ARROGANT	CONVENED	HAMPERED

Red Pony Vocabulary

PARALLEL	ELIMINATED	DRONED	PATERNALLY	PITEOUSLY
STRENUOUSLY	WHETTED	ABRUPTLY	OMINOUSLY	HAMPERED
CONVENED	ARROGANT	FREE SPACE	CONSTRUED	STAUNCHNESS
DISCONSOLATELY	INCENSED	INTRICATELY	IMPERTURBABILITY	CONTEMPLATIVE
PHANTOM	ALOOF	LANGUOROUS	MARTIALLY	NONCHALANCE

Red Pony Vocabulary

ARROGANT	CONTEMPTUOUSLY	PHANTOM	DISCONSOLATELY	LANGUOROUS
ABRUPTLY	DRONED	CONVENED	POTENTIAL	RAMBUNCTIOUSNESS
WHETTED	CONSTRUED	FREE SPACE	RETRACT	STAUNCHNESS
PRESTIGE	LISTLESSLY	PERPETUALLY	INTRICATELY	OMINOUSLY
MARTIALLY	PARALLEL	STRENUOUSLY	PITEOUSLY	NONCHALANCE

Red Pony Vocabulary

ELIMINATED	HAMPERED	PATERNALLY	CONTEMPLATIVE	COMPLACENT
ALOOF	DISPARAGINGLY	IMPERTURBABILITY	VICINITY	NONCHALANCE
PITEOUSLY	STRENUOUSLY	FREE SPACE	MARTIALLY	OMINOUSLY
INTRICATELY	PERPETUALLY	LISTLESSLY	PRESTIGE	STAUNCHNESS
RETRACT	INCENSED	CONSTRUED	WHETTED	RAMBUNCTIOUSNESS

Red Pony Vocabulary

RAMBUNCTIOUSNESS	INCENSED	NONCHALANCE	LISTLESSLY	CONSTRUED
HAMPERED	DISPARAGINGLY	COMPLACENT	STAUNCHNESS	CONVENED
MARTIALLY	PERPETUALLY	FREE SPACE	LANGUOROUS	ABRUPTLY
PITEOUSLY	ALOOF	DRONED	CONTEMPLATIVE	ARROGANT
ELIMINATED	VICINITY	CONTEMPTUOUSLY	PATERNALLY	POTENTIAL

Red Pony Vocabulary

INTRICATELY	PARALLEL	WHETTED	PRESTIGE	OMINOUSLY
STRENUOUSLY	IMPERTURBABILITY	RETRACT	PHANTOM	POTENTIAL
PATERNALLY	CONTEMPTUOUSLY	FREE SPACE	ELIMINATED	ARROGANT
CONTEMPLATIVE	DRONED	ALOOF	PITEOUSLY	ABRUPTLY
LANGUOROUS	DISCONSOLATELY	PERPETUALLY	MARTIALLY	CONVENED

Red Pony Vocabulary

ARROGANT	DISPARAGINGLY	IMPERTURBABILITY	DISCONSOLATELY	PERPETUALLY
RAMBUNCTIOUSNESS	INCENSED	RETRACT	ALOOF	NONCHALANCE
PARALLEL	PRESTIGE	FREE SPACE	PATERNALLY	STRENUOUSLY
HAMPERED	CONTEMPLATIVE	POTENTIAL	LANGUOROUS	STAUNCHNESS
ELIMINATED	LISTLESSLY	WHETTED	MARTIALLY	INTRICATELY

Red Pony Vocabulary

DRONED	CONSTRUED	CONVENED	CONTEMPTUOUSLY	ABRUPTLY
COMPLACENT	PITEOUSLY	OMINOUSLY	PHANTOM	INTRICATELY
MARTIALLY	WHETTED	FREE SPACE	ELIMINATED	STAUNCHNESS
LANGUOROUS	POTENTIAL	CONTEMPLATIVE	HAMPERED	STRENUOUSLY
PATERNALLY	VICINITY	PRESTIGE	PARALLEL	NONCHALANCE

Red Pony Vocabulary

LISTLESSLY	CONTEMPTUOUSLY	POTENTIAL	CONVENED	HAMPERED
INCENSED	ARROGANT	CONSTRUED	LANGUOROUS	PITEOUSLY
RETRACT	ELIMINATED	FREE SPACE	STAUNCHNESS	PERPETUALLY
STRENUOUSLY	ABRUPTLY	CONTEMPLATIVE	OMINOUSLY	RAMBUNCTIOUSNESS
PATERNALLY	VICINITY	COMPLACENT	WHETTED	MARTIALLY

Red Pony Vocabulary

PARALLEL	PRESTIGE	DRONED	IMPERTURBABILITY	NONCHALANCE
INTRICATELY	ALOOF	DISPARAGINGLY	PHANTOM	MARTIALLY
WHETTED	COMPLACENT	FREE SPACE	PATERNALLY	RAMBUNCTIOUSNESS
OMINOUSLY	CONTEMPLATIVE	ABRUPTLY	STRENUOUSLY	PERPETUALLY
STAUNCHNESS	DISCONSOLATELY	ELIMINATED	RETRACT	PITEOUSLY

Red Pony Vocabulary

MARTIALLY	STRENUOUSLY	RETRACT	ABRUPTLY	CONSTRUED
PERPETUALLY	OMINOUSLY	PRESTIGE	HAMPERED	CONVENED
NONCHALANCE	RAMBUNCTIOUSNESS	FREE SPACE	STAUNCHNESS	ARROGANT
DISCONSOLATELY	ALOOF	COMPLACENT	CONTEMPTUOUSLY	LANGUOROUS
INTRICATELY	DRONED	POTENTIAL	PATERNALLY	PARALLEL

Red Pony Vocabulary

INCENSED	PHANTOM	DISPARAGINGLY	CONTEMPLATIVE	LISTLESSLY
VICINITY	ELIMINATED	WHETTED	PITEOUSLY	PARALLEL
PATERNALLY	POTENTIAL	FREE SPACE	INTRICATELY	LANGUOROUS
CONTEMPTUOUSLY	COMPLACENT	ALOOF	DISCONSOLATELY	ARROGANT
STAUNCHNESS	IMPERTURBABILITY	RAMBUNCTIOUSNESS	NONCHALANCE	CONVENED

www.ingramcontent.com/pod-product-compliance
Lightning Source LLC
Chambersburg PA
CBHW081458070526
44586CB00019B/2414